ALANA VALENTINE's work for theatre engages with the authentic real-life stories and voices of Australian communities. Her Currency Press published play *Grounded* won three Australian Writer's Guild Awards in 2013 – in Youth and Community Theatre, the David Williamson Award for Excellence in Theatre Writing, and the Major AWGIE. In 2012, her play *Ear to the Edge of Time* won the International STAGE Script Competition for best new play about science and technology, judged by an esteemed panel of judges that included Nobel laureates and Pulitzer Prize winning authors. *Parramatta Girls* was nominated for two Helpmann Awards – best new Australian work and best play in 2007. It has been on the HSC syllabus for Drama since 2010 and is based on the testimony of former inmates of GTS, Parramatta. The play was remounted by Riverside Theatre in Parramatta in 2014. In 2015 her play about Afghan Australian women, *Shafana and Aunt Sarrinah*, also published by Currency, will go onto the NSW English syllabus. In 2013 the Australia Council for the Arts awarded Alana a Creative Leadership Fellowship to investigate and write about how to gather research material from especially sensitive subjects and she has written about this and her other plays in a memoir called *Writing the Real*. Alana is also the recipient of a NSW Premier's Award, a Queensland Premier's Award, two other AWGIE awards, a Churchill Fellowship and a Centenary of Federation medal.

alanavalentine.com

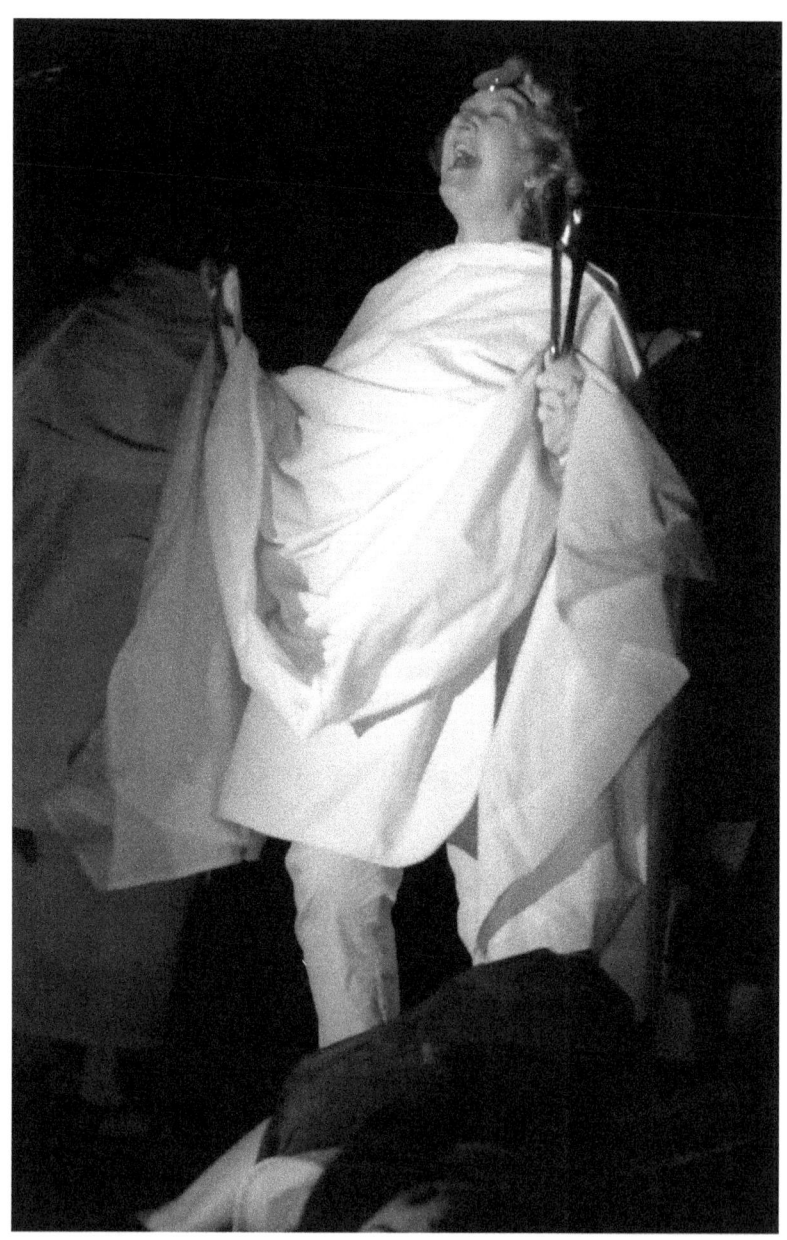

Annie Byron as Gayle in the 2007 Company B production in Sydney. (Photo: Heidrun Löhr)

Parramatta Girls
and
Eyes to the Floor

Alana Valentine

Currency Press,
Sydney

CURRENCY PLAYS

Parramatta Girls first published in 2007
by Currency Press Pty Ltd,
PO Box 2287, Strawberry Hills, NSW, 2012, Australia
enquiries@currency.com.au
www.currency.com.au

This edition published in 2014

Copyright: *Home Girls Have Their Say* © Rosalie Higson, 2007; *Parramatta Girls* © Alana Valentine, 2007; *Eyes to the Floor* © Alana Valentine 2014

COPYING FOR EDUCATIONAL PURPOSES

The Australian Copyright Act 1968 (Act) allows a maximum of one chapter or 10% of this book, whichever is the greater, to be copied by any educational institution for its educational purposes provided that that educational institution (or the body that administers it) has given a remuneration notice to Copyright Agency Limited (CAL) under the Act.

For details of the CAL licence for educational institutions contact CAL, 19/157 Liverpool Street, Sydney, NSW, 2000. Tel: (02) 9394 7600; Fax: (02) 9394 7601; E-mail: info@copyright.com.au

COPYING FOR OTHER PURPOSES

Except as permitted under the Act, for example a fair dealing for the purposes of study, research, criticism or review, no part of this book may be reproduced, stored in a retrieval system, or transmitted in any form or by any means without prior written permission. All enquiries should be made to the publisher at the address above.

Any performance or public reading of Parramatta Girls is forbidden unless a licence has been received from the author or the author's agent. The purchase of this book in no way gives the purchaser the right to perform the play in public, whether by means of a staged production or reading. All applications for public performance should be addressed to: Creative Representation, Level 1, 688 Bourke St, Surry Hills NSW 2010; Ph: 02 9690 5900, F: 02 9690 0980, E: agents@creativerep.com.au

NATIONAL LIBRARY OF AUSTRALIA CIP DATA
  Valentine, Alana, 1961–.
  Parramatta girls and eyes to the floor.
  ISBN 9781925005165 (pbk).
  1. Girls Training School (Parramatta, N.S.W.) – Drama. 2. Girls – Institutional care – New South Wales – Parramatta – Drama. 3. Inmates of institutions – New South Wales – Parramatta – Drama. I. Title.
  A822.3

Cover design by Kate Florance, Currency Press.
Front cover shows Roxanne McDonald as Coral and Jeanette Cronin as Melanie in the 2007 Company B production of *Parramatta Girls*. (Photograph: Heidrun Löhr) Back cover from the 2008 Outback Theatre production of *Eyes to the Floor*. (Photograph: James Edwards)

Contents

Acknowledgements	vi
PARRAMATTA GIRLS	1
Home Girls Have Their Say	
Rosalie Higson	3
Act One	9
Act Two	53
EYES TO THE FLOOR	91
Writer's Note	93
Playscript	97

Currency Press acknowledges the Traditional Owners of the Country on which we live and work. We pay our respects to all Aboriginal and Torres Strait Islander Elders, past and present.

Parramatta Girls
Alana Valentine

ACKNOWLEDGEMENTS

For all those adults who, with great courage and inspirational determination, have survived the experience of childhood in an Australian institution, and especially for those who were incarcerated at GTS Parramatta.

For their honesty, generosity and trust I thank Coral Pombo, Diane O'Brien, Denise Luke, Joyce McBride, Eddie Chatfield, Kerry Roman, Lorraine from Campbelltown, Marlene Riley-Wilson, Christina Riley-Green, Janice Pender, Joan Dale, Valerie Wenberg, Leila Wenberg, Marjorie Woodrow, Jan McGuire, Rita Johnston, Kate Nicholas, Mary Farrell, Carolyn Welsh, Dale Frank, Vicki King, Liz Ebeling, Barbara Denison, Patricia Pedersen, Denise Dravine, Patricia Dawson, Wilma Cassidy, Lynette Aitken, Judi Fraser-Bell, Gail Hannaford, Maree Giles, Bonney Djuric and Melody Mandeno.

And for my grandmother, Joyce Wainwright, whose love was the light of my own childhood years.

Home Girls Have Their Say

Rosalie Higson

Until the 1970s, rebellious or high-spirited teenagers chafed under the threat of being sent to a home for delinquents. For girls, crimes and misdemeanours—playing truant, running off with a boyfriend or mixing with the wrong crowd—could result in a charge of being in moral danger.

Young women from dysfunctional families, which usually meant those with alcoholic parents, were also put away. Thousands between the ages of twelve and eighteen were sentenced and carried the shame of being branded a home girl.

Award-winning writer Alana Valentine has spent four years researching and writing *Parramatta Girls*. The play, written for Company B, is based on the stories of some of the women who served time at the most notorious juvenile centre, the Girls Training School at Parramatta.

The GTS, better known as the Parramatta Girls Home, was closed down in 1974. Its conditions were widely recognised as being even harsher than those adult prisoners endured. Girls frequently rioted because of the punitive, Borstal-like mentality whereby they were kept under surveillance at all times. They scrubbed floors for hours. By the sixties, sentences were usually six to nine months, but in earlier times a girl could spend all her teenage years in the facility.

Sexual and psychological abuse and emotional neglect were commonplace. Drugs such as Valium and Largactil were used to subdue difficult girls, who were frequently placed in isolation, or solitary confinement, for long periods, barefoot, wearing a sack and fed only bread and water.

Valentine, who wrote *Run Rabbit Run* about the supporters of the South Sydney rugby league club, finds great satisfaction in working with real stories.

'I think audiences like that, too,' she says. 'Because everything is so filtered. People want to hear stories about their lives, their back yard, their country.' She first heard about the Parramatta Girls Home in 2003 on an ABC television program that showed some of the former inmates holding a reunion at the old building. 'What has been amazing is that as I researched, I realised that women in the generation above me were all threatened with Parramatta,' Valentine says. 'They'd all heard of it, men and women alike. That astonished me. It's a story that's been waiting to be told for thirty years.'

Over the years, Valentine has come to know some of the women well and says she feels a responsibility to not only make a good drama but to tell the story truthfully, without inflicting any more pain.

'Much of writing the play has been about noticing things, the (lingering) effects of the institution. That's what interested me as much as the raw facts: how they had dealt with that legacy. Lots of people had a tough childhood, and (the incarcerated girls) had a particularly tough childhood: but that's not enough, that's not a play, that's a report.'

Although some people may be empowered by telling their stories, documentary filmmakers and other writers dealing with people's painful memories face ethical questions. 'A lot of (the women) lack self-confidence, have self-esteem issues,' Valentine says. 'They've internalised the idea that they're a bad girl and will never do any good.

'Some women have certainly risen above what they were handed, and we love stories like that, but a lot of them haven't: they are still very damaged. When I was talking to them, they would become that twelve-year-old child. So I had to be very careful.'

When phone calls came from women who wanted to talk about their experiences after forty years of silence, Valentine listened, but did no more interviews. She preferred to talk at length to those who were already part of the informal network of Parramatta girls, so that if they had nightmares, they had other women they could ring and talk to: 'You can't just open up these people and then say, "See ya", because it's really serious stuff.'

With her particular brand of verbatim theatre, Valentine says the trick is to not get seduced by the plot. 'As a dramatist you try and find the things that can't be answered, that can't be resolved. Because that's what life's like. Obviously stuff happens, because it's drama, but small realisations, small understandings, small confessions are huge to these women. It's hopeful because they're so funny, and they deal with their pain in that very Australian way of being very rough and very funny with each other. But ultimately they're making the attempt to understand it.'

As the work developed there were two public readings. At the first, actors read transcripts of the women's stories. 'For the girls the biggest thing was truth-telling,' Valentine says. 'They felt they'd never been heard and never been believed. And I found it hard to get my head around the fact that half the time they didn't know the words for what had happened to them, for what incest was, say. They knew they didn't like it… so the first reading was truth-telling.

'Then we had another reading and I included guard characters and family characters, and Neil Armfield (Artistic Director of Company B) came up to me and said, "We're not interested in other people, we're interested in the women."

'I thought that was right. A play about why people are sadistic, malicious bastards is another play altogether.'

Anyone who has seen the old buildings in Parramatta will know how intimidating and depressing they are: 'The place has a long history, beginning with the Female Factory just next door to the girls home, which was originally an orphanage,' Valentine says. 'They would take the babies when they were three and put them in the orphanage. In 1887 it became an industrial school for girls and remained a home through to 1974. Now it's the Norma Parker Detention Centre for Women.

'This is the site of almost continuous female incarceration in Australia, since the first white people came here. So what is the philosophy behind incarcerating girls? Girls shouldn't step outside the norm, shouldn't be oversexed, they have to be taught how to be a proper woman.'

Juvenile detention statistics show that the boys and girls are overwhelmingly from poor backgrounds. Some of the women Valentine met were from middle-class families, but they were the exception that proves the rule, she says. 'The women are mostly what I would call battlers, and they continue to be that. Again, that's an indictment. Why, when those girls are uncontrollable, do we lock them up and make them scrub floors? Is it because that's what they're going to do later?'

Some of the women Valentine met had got through their time at

Parramatta fairly unscathed: 'It was hard, but it was okay,' they said. Valentine told them, 'Look, I'm not just going for the salacious kind of headlines; I want to know the full thing.' That involved being addressed by their numbers rather than their names, horrible haircuts, being forced to scrub and perform other domestic duties and, for many decades, missing out on education.

Early in her research Valentine attended hearings at Parramatta of a Senate inquiry, called 'Forgotten Australians', that investigated the experiences of those who were in institutional or out-of-home care as children. The notorious Parramatta Girls Home had lived up to its reputation.

'The thing that shocked me the most was the routine physical examination when girls entered the home, to determine whether or not they were virgins. That could have nothing to do with why they were in there: even if they were charged with neglect, or being uncontrollable, or had alcoholic parents, they were given the examination. At the Senate inquiry I saw a doctor who said he had to do it and resented being used by the State in this way.'

The Senate report estimated that 500,000 children were put in care in the past century in this country, Valentine says. 'And that means that every person is related to, lives next door to or has some relationship to a child who was put into care.'

This article first appeared in The Australian
19 March 2007.

Parramatta Girls was first produced by Company B at the Belvoir Street Theatre, Sydney, on 17 March 2007, with the following cast:

LYNETTE	Valerie Bader
GAYLE	Annie Byron
MELANIE	Jeanette Cronin
KERRY	Lisa Flanagan
MAREE	Genevieve Hegney
CORAL	Roxanne McDonald
MARLENE	Leah Purcell
JUDI	Carole Skinner

Director, Wesley Enoch
Set Designer, Ralph Myers
Costume Designer, Alice Babidge
Lighting Designer, Rachel Burke
Sound Designer, Steve Francis

CHARACTERS

MARLENE, 13/57, indigenous
JUDI, 16/59, non-indigenous
MELANIE, 15/58, non-indigenous
LYNETTE, 14/57, non-indigenous
KERRY, 15/58, indigenous
GAYLE, 16/59, non-indigenous
MAREE, 14, non-indigenous
CORAL, 16/58, indigenous

SETTING

The play is set in 2003, and the remembered past.

ACT ONE

SCENE ONE

MAREE, *dressed in a Parramatta Girls uniform, sits on stage, amongst the pile of detritus. She exits when* JUDY *enters.*

JUDI *addresses the audience.*

JUDI: Me and my brother used to build billycarts. You know, just basically a board with wheels on it that we'd nick off old prams or so. One time we used the wheels off of a shopping trolley. And we'd fix them onto the board and there you had your billycart. Once we got some black and painted the board and we called that bugger, it was a big bugger too, we called that the hearse. And, see, we lived up the top of a hill. So the biggest thrill we could get was to get on the cart and just career down the hill. Just fly. I can remember just flyin' down the road, arms out, the wind makin' my eyes water, laughin' and screamin' with everyone watchin' ya. Now, at the bottom of the hill was a main road. Which was fine because you'd just, you know, use the rope attached to the front wheels to pull the wheels to the side. Which could be hard when you were at, you know, top speed, but you just pulled hard on one side and spun around to avoid any car that might be coming. So you'd belt down the hill, yank the rope and kinda skid around on a one-eighty at the bottom.

And that was fine, all part of the thrill, you know. And, look, your elbows used to take a bit of a battering and this was before they invented, what are they called, the elbow pads, [*tapping her own forehead*] thank you. So you used to scrape your elbows a bit, pretty regular. Scrape off a bit of skin, bit of blood. That's all right, all part of bein' a kid, isn't it? But after a while I kinda found that the wounds on my elbows wouldn't heal. And we didn't have the money to go to the doctor even if I'd ever thought of asking to, which I didn't, and I just thought it would heal, you know. But as time went on they just kinda stayed a little bit wet and open, and they didn't get infected at all, they just sort of stayed raw and painful. And eventually when I got put in the home, they put this stuff on them and they healed a bit. But if we had to do scrubbing or stuff, or laundry, or all the work we had to do because they made us work really hard in there, every now and then they'd just start up bleeding again and I'd have to put this sorta white powder on them which stang, you know.

And eventually they healed, I mean, I still have to be careful with them. Like, they're healed, but if I knock them or something I get… bloody, I dunno what I get… I guess, I wonder if this time they won't… you know… this time they won't heal up. Like, I never knew, I never knew that elbows could just never heal up. Ya just rely on things ta scab up, don't you? And you don't realise how much you use your elbows until you've got something like this and if you use them the scab breaks all over again.

She rolls up her sleeves and shows her bandaged elbows.

Now you can laugh, this is funny, you can laugh that I've taped up my elbows today. As if anyone is going to knock them. I mean, they haven't been bad for years, for forty years, which is about how long since I've been back to the place. For forty years they've been fine. Common or garden variety elbows. I check them all the time and it's just stupid. [*Beat.*] I just don't want to be sittin' there, drinkin' me tea with these girls, and suddenly have wet elbows. You know, someone might say, 'What's that?', and I just don't know that I want to have to explain it. These weird, weeping elbows, you know. 'Bloody hell, she's a queer one.'

So, I'll go today, and geez I'm looking forward to seeing them girls. But I have strapped up my elbows, just in case.

> JUDI *remains on stage, as lights come up on the courtyard of the Parramatta Girls Home. There is the shadow of a large, ironwork gate on stage. Women wait to enter the home for a reunion. It is the first time many of them have been inside the home since they were incarcerated here as teenagers. The mood is agitated, expectant. Some women are pacing.*

GAYLE: Hi.
JUDI: Hello.

There is an uncomfortable silence.

GAYLE: So when were you here?
JUDI: 1961. You?
GAYLE: 1961. [*Pause.*] It'll be smaller than we remember.
JUDI: Reckon it will be.
GAYLE: Do you think the dungeons will still be there?
JUDI: You mean the isolation block?
GAYLE: No, the dungeons.

Behind her, MELANIE *is greeting* CORAL *with hello and a hug.*

JUDI: There were never any dungeons.
GAYLE: Well, I remember them.
JUDI: It was never that bad. [*Beat.*] It was harsh but it wasn't all bad.

They look at each other. There is another uncomfortable silence.
GAYLE *moves away.* MELANIE *speaks to* CORAL.

MELANIE: You nervous about going in today, Coral?
CORAL: No. [*Beat.*] But I put extra glue in me dentures anyway, Melanie.

CORAL *laughs, nervous.*

MELANIE: What'd they put you in here for, Coral?
CORAL: Uncontrollable.
CORAL & MELANIE: [*together*] Exposed to moral danger.
MELANIE: Still. Ya musta done something ta end up in here.
CORAL: What?
MELANIE: [*ironically*] Ya musta deserved it.
CORAL: Yeah, something really serious, Melanie.
MELANIE: Like skipping school.
CORAL: Like you could scratch your bum the wrong way in those days and be considered uncontrollable.

They laugh. Pause.

[*Shaking her head*] Uncontrollable, eh?
MELANIE: The first time I was put in here it was for being uncontrollable. Then I escaped. Hitched a ride to Woy Woy. Got involved with this bloke. Stood lookout while he did a service station. Both of us got done. They put me back here.

CORAL *continues to walk around.*

CORAL: Y'all right, Kerry?

KERRY: I'll be all right, Coral.
CORAL: They got counsellors here.
KERRY: Now what have I ever done to you?
CORAL: What?
KERRY: To deserve you sicking some counsellor on me.
CORAL: I'm just saying, Kerry. They're there if ya want them.
GAYLE: Who are the counsellors, then?
KERRY: That girl over there. I think she's one.

She gestures to an unseen girl across the stage.

She must be all of twenty-five.
CORAL: Maybe she can tell us who started this whole mess.
KERRY: Nah, she wasn't even born when they thought of this place.
MELANIE: None of us were.

They all look up at the gate. Another woman, MARLENE, *joins them.*

MARLENE: Burramatta.
GAYLE: What, Marlene?
MARLENE: The Burramattagal clan of the Dhurug. Burramatta.
CORAL: Parramatta.

Pause.

KERRY: 1796 they built a place here for the female convicts.
GAYLE: Yeah, I knew that. The Female Factory, right?
MARLENE: That's the one next door, Gayle.
KERRY: Turned that into a loony bin eventually.
CORAL: Took their convict babies away and put them in the orphanage when they turned three.
MELANIE: And that was our building. From when?
KERRY: You wanna know?
GAYLE: Yeah. I wanna know.
MARLENE: Be careful what ya ask for.
MELANIE: 'Cause Kerry'll tell ya dates.
KERRY: 1841.
CORAL: Government orphanage.
KERRY: 1844? [*Pause.*] Catholic orphanage. 1887?
MELANIE: Girls Industrial School.
KERRY: 1912.

MARLENE & CORAL: [*together*] Girls Training Home.
KERRY: 1925.
GAYLE: Parramatta Girls Home.
KERRY: 1946, Girls Training School Parramatta. 1974, Kamballa Girls Institution. 1980, Norma Parker Detention Centre for Women… to the present day.
MARLENE: And why do you think they kept changing the names, Gayle?
KERRY: Because they'd have an enquiry that would say shut it down. So they would shut it down. Technically. Just change the name and you've shut it down.
GAYLE: Bloody hell!
MELANIE: Watch it, ya foul mouthed little bitch, or we'll wash your mouth out with soap.

There is a moment, then it relaxes when MELANIE *pulls a face.*

GAYLE: Why do you know all that?
KERRY: They're the facts.
GAYLE: But that's…
KERRY: … what comes of not bein' believed.
GAYLE: When have you not been believed?
KERRY: Start yesterday and work backwards.
GAYLE: By who?
KERRY: No one important, really. Oh, there's the government enquiries into this place that did nothing. And you may as well throw in the courts that have never charged no one associated with this place with any crime. Just them. Unless you want to add every person who doesn't want to hear how bad it was. Yeah, if you counted all of them then I'd say this, today, is the first day I ever been listened to about this place.
MELANIE: Fancy you got yourself a bit of an 'historic occasion', Kerry. Have ya?

They laugh. Pause.

GAYLE: That what you think, Marlene?
MARLENE: Me? I just think it's an opportunity to shake hands with them ol' demons.

MARLENE *shakes hands with* MELANIE.

CORAL: Nearly every 'delinquent' girl in the history of Australia has been through here at some time or another.

MARLENE: So it's gonna be one helluva fun reunion, eh!

They laugh. A long silence.

I really wanted to just...

GAYLE: See it.

CORAL: See it again. [*Pause.*] The first day I was here I heard a girl screaming and they told me that the other girls... that something was being done to her with a toilet brush and I shouldn't get involved. So I didn't. And I kept my head down from then on.

GAYLE: So you were all right.

CORAL: Well. Except that that's how I then went through life.

GAYLE: You mean never... protesting, like.

CORAL: [*bitter*] Protecting myself.

Pause.

MARLENE: How long do we have to stand out here, do you think?

CORAL: Oh, they'll keep us waiting, Marlene. Just to remind us.

KERRY *goes over to the 'gate'.*

KERRY: I would have come up to about there on this.

CORAL: We was smaller then.

MARLENE: I was thirteen when I first went in.

GAYLE: I was fourteen. But I was a scrawny bugger.

JUDI: Just a little girl, really.

MELANIE: Just a pack of scrawny buggers.

KERRY: Thought I knew everything.

CORAL: I bloody did know everything.

MARLENE: I bloody still do.

They laugh.

MELANIE: Thought I could escape.

KERRY: But even if you climbed the wall, there was still the gate.

CORAL: There was.

MARLENE: Big spikes on top of it.

They all stand looking at the 'gate'.

GAYLE: Come on. They're lettin' us in.

KERRY, JUDI *and* GAYLE *and* CORAL *exit.*

The lights change. MARLENE *and* MELANIE *huddle on stage.*

MELANIE: What's your name, then?
MARLENE: Marlene.
MELANIE: We've got to get out of the car.
MARLENE: No, this place must be for you.
MELANIE: What?
MARLENE: This place.
MELANIE: Come on, she's telling us both to get out, Marlene.
MARLENE: I'm not getting out.
MELANIE: You'd better.

> MELANIE *stands.* MARLENE *stands as if wrenched to her feet.*

Told you it was both.
MARLENE: But there must be a mistake.
MELANIE: Save it.

> MARLENE *is backing back.*

MARLENE: I'm not going in there. [*She reacts as if she has been struck.*] Ow!
MELANIE: Come on.
MARLENE: I'm not going…

> MARLENE *continues to struggle, reacting as if she's getting dragged along, screaming.*

I want to see my mum.

> *The two girls exit.*
>
> *The lights find* LYNETTE, *breathing deeply. After a moment she begins to take everything out of her bag. She is making a pile of rubbish papers, folding up receipts, sorting out her money.* MAREE *enters. She wears a Parramatta Girls uniform.*

MAREE: Do you have to do that now?

> *Pause.*

LYNETTE: I just thought… while we're waiting to go in… I'd…
MAREE: You shouldn't be flashing your money around.
LYNETTE: I'm not.
MAREE: You are. And you shouldn't around these sort of women.

> *Pause.*

LYNETTE: You weren't in here with the rest of us, then?
MAREE: I was in here. That's why I'm saying it.

Valerie Bader as Lynette in the 2007 Company B production in Sydney. (Photo: Heidrun Löhr)

LYNETTE: Lynette.
MAREE: Maree.
LYNETTE: I was in here with a Maree. [*She looks into the middle distance, as though remembering her past.*] So you think they'd…
MAREE: They didn't come from the North Shore then and they don't come from the North Shore now.

LYNETTE *finishes putting the things away in her purse.*

You coming, Lynette?
LYNETTE: Nah. I'm just gonna stay here for a bit, Maree.
MAREE: You sure?
LYNETTE: Yeah. I'll be in in a mo.
MAREE: See ya in there, then.
LYNETTE: Yeah. See you in there. [*Beat.*] I'd never come across girls like that before. I mean, I went to St Catherine's at Waverley and all the girls there were very posh… and, you know, good backgrounds, and my background was very solid in that way as well… I just had never come across girls like that before. I mean, their knowledge of sex, their knowledge of drugs and alcohol and abuse, the things that they'd been subjected to by their families. I sort of felt that I was not so much better, but just completely different to them, so it was really hard for me to relate to anybody as well. And then this girl Maree befriended me. She was a friend to me. She really was.

LYNETTE *sits on stage, fussing with her purse.*

SCENE TWO

A group of women enter the home.

CORAL: This way, ladies. DOCS would like you to sign in the visitors book. Then you can go exploring around the home wherever you like.
MARLENE: I'm not signing their book. They got enough records on me. [*Beat.*] Oooh.
CORAL: Can you smell it? It's the old processing cell.
MARLENE: They dragged me through here. Out of the black car. Black tinted windows. Into that processing cell.

The group exits.

On another part of the stage, GAYLE *and* JUDI *enter, as older women.*

GAYLE: My file had two lines on it.

JUDI: What's that?

GAYLE: That's the number of fingers the doctor was able to insert.

JUDI: Maybe it was something else.

GAYLE: It wasn't something else. It was the number of fingers. Two lines, two fingers. If he could get two in that meant you were still a virgin, if he could get three in you'd had sex, if he could get four in, well. I've never met anyone with four lines on their file. Have you?

JUDI: No, and I don't believe—

GAYLE: My daughter said don't go down into the dungeons. It won't do you any good. But I want to go down and look at them. I want to see those dungeons. I want to see them again with my own eyes.

JUDI: There weren't any dungeons. And there's no way guards could have assaulted anyone. They wouldn't have jeopardised their jobs. And they were always with another guard. There was no place down below, no dungeon. It's memory playing tricks on you.

GAYLE: There were.

JUDI: Well, I was in here for four years and I don't remember 'em.

GAYLE: What would you know?

Pause.

JUDI: I'd know.

GAYLE: Yeah, you'd know. You'd know everything.

JUDI: What did you say?

GAYLE: You'd know everything. Little Miss Smarty Pants.

JUDI: Do I know you?

GAYLE: I didn't twig to what was happening at all. Did not twig. You used to get taken away into the building and we'd wonder. I can remember your attitude of being superior than everyone. I thought if you showed your face here today I'd have—

JUDI: What's your name?

GAYLE: Don't pretend you don't know. You know who I am. Like I know who you are.

JUDI: My name is Judi.

GAYLE: I know who you are, Fay McKell. Don't think I don't know you. You were his favourite. [*Loudly*] She was giving it away to the Superintendent. At fifteen. Knew how to work it to her advantage even then.

    GAYLE *sort of pushes* JUDI. JUDI *pushes her back.*

JUDI: Don't you dare push me.

    CORAL, *as older, comes over.*

CORAL: Come on now. Stop this. This reunion is for all of us.

GAYLE: She knew what she was doing, Coral. She was smart. And she was stuck-up.

JUDI: I don't know what she's talking about.

    GAYLE *and* JUDI *exit.* CORAL *watches.*

    MELANIE *and* MARLENE, *as children, are in the admissions cell.*

MELANIE: [*singing*] Charlotte the harlot lay dying,
    Three pisspots supported her head,
    Three poofters around her lay crying,
    And she turned on her left tit and said,
    I've been fucked by the Germans and Russians,
    By the Chinese and Japanese too.
    But I come back to good old Australia
    To be fucked by old bastards like you.
 Know any jokes?

MARLENE: What?

MELANIE: Jokes. Preferably dirty ones.

MARLENE: That's disgusting.

MELANIE: Not as disgusting as this place. Trust me.

MARLENE: Have you been here before?

MELANIE: Do roos shit in the bush?

MARLENE: Don't say shit.

MELANIE: [*singing*] So roll back your dirty old foreskins
    And give me the juice from your nuts.
    So they rolled back their dirty old foreskins
    And whitewashed the walls of her guts.

MARLENE: Stop it.

MELANIE: Why? It upsets the guards.

MARLENE: Why do you want to upset them?

MELANIE: I just do.

MARLENE: Well, I don't. I shouldn't even be in here.
MELANIE: You won't last ten minutes in here.
MARLENE: Good. Then they'll put me somewhere else.
MELANIE: Yeah, like the asylum next door. That's where they put you if you don't fit in here.

Pause.

MARLENE: What's your name?
MELANIE: Melanie.
MARLENE: Just be quiet, Melanie. Just stop your filthy mouth.
MELANIE: And who's going to stop me?
MARLENE: I am.
MELANIE: I thought you weren't even supposed to be in here.
MARLENE: I'm not.
MELANIE: Then stop acting like you run the joint.
MARLENE: Then stop trying to scare me more than I already am.

MELANIE looks at her. MARLENE looks like she's going to start crying.

MELANIE: Don't.
MARLENE: What?
MELANIE: Lose your bottle.
MARLENE: My what?
MELANIE: You know. Don't let it drip out your arse.

Pause. MARLENE laughs despite herself.

MARLENE: Where'd you hear that stuff?
MELANIE: Me dad's a wobbly.
MARLENE: A wobbly arse?
MELANIE: Not a wobbly arse. They're anarchists. Anti-state.
MARLENE: The what?
MELANIE: Just anti. [*Beat.*] Anti, you know. Anti.

MARLENE nods.

MARLENE: So, did they come get you?
MELANIE: Nah. I ran away from home.
MARLENE: You ran away?
MELANIE: Yeah. So?
MARLENE: I'd never do that. [*Pause.*] How long do we have to stay in this room?

MELANIE: Until they assign us a dorm.
MARLENE: Then what?
MELANIE: Then you get to meet Doctor Fingers.
Pause.
MARLENE: Why do they call him that?
MELANIE: Because he's got dirty, great big fingers that he sticks into you.
MARLENE: I don't believe you.
MELANIE: First thing he'll say to you is, 'Get up on the table. How many times have you been fucked?'
MARLENE: A doctor would never say that.
MELANIE: Then he shoves it in.
MARLENE: He does not.
MELANIE: We call it the duck's bill. He really shoves it, too.
MARLENE: Why would he do that?
MELANIE: Checking for crabs.
MARLENE: What sort of crabs?
MELANIE: Public lice.
MARLENE: What?
MELANIE: VD. Don't you know anything?
MARLENE: What's VD stand for? Victory Day?
Pause.
MELANIE: Very Dumb. Did I say you wouldn't last ten minutes in here? Make that five.
MARLENE: If I behave myself I'll be fine. If I follow the rules they'll treat me fairly.

> MELANIE *exits, laughing.*
>
> MARLENE *is repeating 'If I behave myself I'll be fine; if I follow the rules they'll treat me fairly' like a mantra. She walks forward and, still wearing her dress, removes her underpants. She lays down on the floor and parts her legs. Then she turns her head to the side and cries as her legs move further apart.* GAYLE *comes on, dressed as the* DOCTOR, *in a white sheet. All the other girls surround her and chime in as the* DOCTOR *'examines'* MARLENE.

DOCTOR: This is to certify that I have examined Marlene Kenneally and find her to be of sound physique and free from signs of active organic disease, or of venereal disease. She is *non virgo intacta* and the appearances suggest frequent penetration.

MARLENE: That's not true. That's just not true.

GAYLE: The doctor says you're a little slut.

MARLENE: Get away from me. Get away.

> MARLENE *stands.* GAYLE *is struggling with her when the girls all turn to enact a mock trial which is part Alice in Wonderland and partly the reality of the Children's Court in Darlinghurst in the 1960s.*
>
> *One of the girls has a judge's gavel and she bangs it on something hard. They wear sheets as gowns and mop heads as wigs.*

PLAYER: Children's Court, Darlinghurst, is in session.

PLAYER: The court will come to order.

> *Two of the girls grab* MARLENE *and hold her. The* JUDGE *is sitting on a chair.*

PLAYER: You are charged with being uncontrollable. And there's only one place to send you to make you properly disciplined.

> *The two girls holding her call out.*

PLAYERS: Send her to Parramatta!

MARLENE: No. I haven't done anything wrong. They took away my brothers and sister, they told me I would have to be charged.

PLAYER: With neglect.

MARLENE: Who did I neglect?

JUDGE: You are charged with being neglected.

MARLENE: But how can you charge me with neglect?

PLAYER: I think you can see, Your Honour, that this girl's mental capacity is one of the impediments to her understanding simple moral concepts.

JUDGE: Yes, I see that.

PLAYER: She is, and I quote from her official file, 'She is somewhat mentally retarded'.

MARLENE: I am not mentally retarded.

JUDGE: Silence.

MARLENE: But I'm not—

PLAYER: Your Honour can see what happens when a rebellious spirit is housed in the female body and that is coupled with the disadvantage

of a none-too mentally acute mind.
JUDGE: Yes. Yes. I see.
PLAYERS: Send her to Parramatta.
MARLENE: No.
PLAYERS: Send her to Parramatta.
MARLENE: Stop it. Stop it.

> *She continues crying out 'Stop it' and then stands on stage, tears in her eyes.*
>
> *The women remove the sheets and mop heads. They are wearing white nightshirts and carrying small white bed sheets.*

GIRLS: [*singing*] The water is wide, I cannot get o'er,
Neither have I the wings to fly,
Give me a boat that can carry two,
And both shall row, my love and I.

A ship there is and she sails the sea,
She's loaded deep as deep can be,
But not so deep as the love I'm in,
I know not if I sink or swim.

> MELANIE *has a mop and an iron bucket. While staring at* GAYLE, *she hands* MARLENE *a mop.* MELANIE *drops the bucket with a bang.*

MARLENE: What?
MELANIE: Just do it.
MARLENE: What?
MELANIE: Mop.

> MARLENE *takes the mop, squeezes out some water and mops the stage.* GAYLE *moves in front of her and spits on the floor where* MARLENE *has just mopped.*

Leave her alone.

> GAYLE *turns to look at* MELANIE.

GAYLE: Says who?
MELANIE: Says me.
GAYLE: Your number's not even dry yet.
MELANIE: I don't care if me new number's not even dry.
MARLENE: What are you doing?

MELANIE: Shut up, I'm dealing with it.
GAYLE: You know who I am, don't you?
MELANIE: Dunno, are ya the Queen of England? I heard she was an ugly-looking bint.
GAYLE: Don't speak to me like that.
MELANIE: Or what?
GAYLE: Or you'll get into trouble with the officers.
MELANIE: You their lap dog, are ya?
GAYLE: Someone has to keep the girls in line.
MELANIE: Is that what they call it?
GAYLE: House Captain is what they call it.
MELANIE: Bum suck is what I call it.
GAYLE: You're asking for it, Woodrow.
MARLENE: Melanie, just forget it.
MELANIE: You know, my father used to say to me, if there's a mob of 'em, hit the one with the biggest mouth.

> *Suddenly,* MELANIE *hits* GAYLE *in the face with the iron bucket. The girls attack and struggle with* MELANIE *and* MARLENE. JUDI *and* CORAL *enter, as older women.*

CORAL: What are you doin' out here?
JUDI: I'm leavin'.
CORAL: How come?
JUDI: Just 'cause I can.
CORAL: But they haven't done the speeches yet or nothin'.
JUDI: This doesn't change what they did. None of 'em are here to make amends. It's just a bunch of miserable old girls rakin' over the past.

> *Pause.*

CORAL: Last time us girls got together we went down The Rocks for a big feed. Gala dinner they called it.
JUDI: Don't start, Coral, I wanna go.
CORAL: We hired this bus, to take us out to Picton where we were havin' the reunion.
JUDI: Coral—
CORAL: So we get on, about fifty blackfella women and our driver, he's Pakistani, lovely fella but he's only had his bus licence for maybe a day. I reckon the bus company went, oh, yeah, pack of old ducks, we'll give 'em the rookie, see. So we finish our meal and have a

few drinks and by the time he gets to us he needs to get us home in a bit of a hurry so that he can stop and do his prayers. And he's got a friend with him too, another Pakistani fella, and 'e's standing in the entrance well, talking to him while he drives.

JUDI: Right under the sign that says 'Do not stand, do not speak to driver'.

CORAL: That's the one. So the girls pile on and one of 'em shouts out, let's go up the Cross.

JUDI: And he's got no idea how to get there.

CORAL: No idea. So the girls say, 'Coral will direct you.'

    JUDI *is laughing a bit now.*

So they shove me down the front. Suddenly I'm the Queen of Bohemia, you know. Anyways, I direct him up through the city.

JUDI: Well done.

CORAL: Soon as we hit the bottom of William Street, I get on the microphone they use to give tour information, and I start doin' a

From left: Jeanette Cronin as Melanie, Annie Byron as Gayle and Genevieve Hegney as Maree in the 2007 Company B production in Sydney. (Photo: Heidrun Löhr)

runnin' commentary of the Cross.

Ah… 'Okay, there are some girls out for the night, g'day girls.' And we all wave at them, this pack of fifty old blackfella women starin' out of the bus screamin' and cacklin' like we're fit to be tied. 'And there's a customer, his dick's the size of your car's pop-out cigarette lighter. And there's this famous brothel, there's that famous brothel.' And the two Pakistanis have their eyes bulging out of their heads, the one who's driving couldn't drive the bus before, and here we are, creepin' down the Kings Cross road, a pack of out-of-control Parramatta Girls, as if we own the place. This enormous bus wedged into that little street and the neon's flashin' and the security guards are wavin' and I laughed, I laughed 'til I was cryin' is how I laughed. And I looked around and all the girls they had tears running down their faces they were laughin' so much.

JUDI and CORAL are killing themselves laughing.

And it was worth more than fifty talks for fifty years with any counsellor. Do you know what I'm sayin'?

JUDI just looks at her.

Then go back inside.

JUDI nods and exits.

The lights change and KERRY *enters, carrying scrubbing brushes.* CORAL *and* KERRY *begin to scrub the covered way.*

KERRY: See that?
CORAL: What?
KERRY: Don't look up.
CORAL: Well, how am I supposed to see it if I don't look up?
KERRY: Well, you see it every day so you shouldn't have to look at it now.
CORAL: What?
KERRY: The lemon tree.
CORAL: Yeah. So.
KERRY: Don't look up at it.
CORAL: Why not? It's a lemon tree.
KERRY: Yeah. Well, it's going to get us into sick bay.
CORAL: For what?
KERRY: For cream, and maybe more.

CORAL: Oh. [*Beat.*] How?
KERRY: You know how we rubbed toothpaste on our lips so that they'd get chapped and we'd get more cream?
CORAL: Yeah.
KERRY: Well, Maree reckons lemon is even better. It really dries out your skin.
CORAL: So we can get more cream to rub into it?
KERRY: Yeah.
CORAL: But if we don't rub the lemon or the toothpaste into it to make it all dry then why do we need the cream?
KERRY: So's we can go sick bay.
CORAL: And?
KERRY: And from sick bay we might be able to get out of here. And escape.
CORAL: Escape?
KERRY: So we've got to get a lemon.
CORAL: Okay.
KERRY: So. Way you go.
CORAL: Me?
KERRY: Yeah.
CORAL: Why me?
KERRY: You know that last week Gayle scaled the wall trying to get out of here.
CORAL: Yeah.
KERRY: And Maree once put a pin in her arm and she was rushed to hospital when it travelled to her heart.
CORAL: Wow!
KERRY: Yeah. I've tried sticking pins in my legs.
CORAL: Where?
KERRY: Here. Here's the scar.

    CORAL *examines the scar on* KERRY*'s leg.*

CORAL: It looks like one-seven-one.
KERRY: It is one-seven-one. For a girl.
CORAL: What girl?
KERRY: No one. Come on, ya wanna escape, don't ya?

    They continue to scrub.

CORAL: I'm not getting that lemon.

KERRY: Do it, or I'll…
CORAL: You'll what?
KERRY: I'll get you back.
CORAL: [*suddenly shouting*] I'm not doing nothing no one tells me ever again.
> KERRY *looks at her, shocked.*

KERRY: What are you on about?
CORAL: I just don't want to.
KERRY: All right. Fine.
> *They exit.*

SCENE THREE

LYNETTE *gets up to go in. Then can't.*

LYNETTE: Every time I smell something that reminds me, or see something that reminds me, it's like the devil's got hold of one arm and God's gotta hold of the other and they start to pull. And I start to tear right down deep in my groin and they keep pulling and they tear my guts in half and they tear my womb in half and they tear my lungs in half. And it's like I want them to pull harder, pull harder so that they tear my heart in half and tear out my throat and split my jaw and separate my eyes. And that's what every memory of being a child is like. There's no safe place to go back to. It's just the minute I start to remember, the tearing in half begins. And the minute I walked in that gate, that's when the tearing started up again.
> GAYLE *is in the shower area. She hears the sound of a ghost whistle and she stands at attention.*

GAYLE: Present.
> *There is the ghostly echo of another whistle. Then there is an echoing reverberant sound of showers being turned on.*

> GAYLE *begins to take off her shoes and stockings. She removes her skirt and is standing in her top with her underpants half down when* MAREE *enters. There are scars visible, all over her legs. Strange whirls and patches.*

MAREE: You all right, luv?
GAYLE: I have to have a shower.

Pause.

MAREE: No, luv. No you don't have to have a shower.

GAYLE: I have to have a shower! [*She is jumping up and down.*] Dance of the jiggly tit. It makes the guards laugh.

MAREE: You don't have to have a shower.

GAYLE: Have you had your shower?

MAREE: No, we're not having showers today.

GAYLE: We don't have to have a shower today?

MAREE: No.

GAYLE *looks at her.*

GAYLE: But we have to have a shower every day.

MAREE: No, but not today.

GAYLE: I'll only shower for two minutes. Do you have long showers?

MAREE: Well, no. Now that you mention it.

GAYLE: See. That's it. That's their mark that you can't wash off.

She is scrubbing away at her skin, trying to wash off an imaginary mark.

MAREE: But I could have long showers if I wanted to. And so can you. When you go home.

GAYLE: But I won't.

MAREE: All right.

GAYLE: Do you have baths?

MAREE: No.

GAYLE: See. That's it. That's their mark that you can't wash off.

Pause. GAYLE *suddenly realises what she is doing and hurriedly puts back on her clothes.*

MAREE: Listen, luv, are you all right? Is there someone here with you?

Pause.

GAYLE: I was made to sleep in the car with a blanket and pillow in the middle of winter and I was frightened of spiders. I can always remember finding this spider in the back of this old Vauxhall, or whatever it was, that belonged to George. I don't want to call him my father. I'll call him George because he was never a father to me. So from that day to this day I've been terrified of spiders... I got in... I had to sleep in the car one night and this spider crawled across my face... and I raced into my... p... [*she gags on the word 'parents'*] ... so-called step mother and father and told them what was in the car. My father hit me so much that he kicked me on the ground and I had a slipped disc and I couldn't walk for three weeks. I was a kid, a kid, a kid. I would have been about fourteen. People don't believe me.

MAREE: I believe you. [*Beat.*] Why don't we go upstairs into the courtyard?

GAYLE: I don't want to go home.

MAREE: No, you don't have to go home. Let's just get some fresh air for a minute. Then you can come back down here if you want.

> MAREE *and* GAYLE *exit.*
>
> KERRY *enters. She is carrying two large pots of mashed potato. She begins to mash one with an enormous potato masher.* MARLENE *picks up the masher, as if she has never done any kitchen work in her life.*

KERRY: Not like that. Mash it.

> MARLENE *mashes harder.*

Put your back into it. Imagine it's someone you really want to pulverise.

> MARLENE *is mashing but isn't very convincing.*

That's not pulverise. That's just someone you want to give a massage to.

MARLENE: It's breaking my arm.

KERRY: No, this is breaking your arm.

> KERRY *puts* MARLENE'S *arm up behind her back.*

MARLENE: Ow.

KERRY: Now. Mash the potatoes.

> MARLENE *mashes, much more powerfully.*

KERRY: Good. I suppose that's my head you're crushing.

MARLENE: You better believe it.

KERRY: Good.

> KERRY *then takes the masher out of the potatoes and flicks a big gob of mash at* MARLENE. KERRY *immediately flicks some back. They begin a mashed potato fight. They are laughing and carrying on.* MARLENE *squeals and* KERRY *puts her hand over her face.*

Just don't squeal, okay?

> MARLENE *nods. As soon as* KERRY *releases her,* MARLENE *squeals again. This time* KERRY *struggles to get her hand over her mouth.*

I told you not to squeal. And I didn't do it for my amusement. If you get the officers in here you'll really find out about someone you'd like to pulverise. Now promise me you won't squeal.

> MARLENE *nods.*

Promise or I'll shove your face in this hot mash and, believe me, I'll do it.

> MARLENE *looks scared and nods.*

I'm sorry I had to say that but if you get the Matron in here we're finished.

MARLENE: What do you mean finished?

> *She hands her a towel and* MARLENE *cleans herself up.* KERRY *wipes some potato off* MARLENE*'s face. They mash in silence.*

KERRY: What are you in here for, anyway?

MARLENE: Neglect.

KERRY: So how long did you get?

MARLENE: Six months. How 'bout you?

KERRY: Oh. I'm a State Ward. They charged me with being uncontrollable at three months old.

MARLENE: So how long have you been here?

KERRY: Here? Six months, three to go. The terms are mostly six and nine.

MARLENE: Why's that?

> KERRY *shrugs.*

KERRY: Length of a pregnancy, I guess. [*Pause.*] I've been in Bidura, Cootamundra Girls Home, here at Parramatta, couple of foster homes. Are you doin' all right?

MARLENE: 'Course I am. This place doesn't scare me.

KERRY: That's good. 'Cause it scares the bloody living daylights out of me.

> *They continue to mash in silence.*

My last foster home, up in Moree, I was only allowed to go to the cemetery on a Sund'y.

Lisa Flanagan (left) as Kerry and Leah Purcell as Marlene in the 2007 Company B production in Sydney. (Photo: Heidrun Löhr)

MARLENE: What d'ya mean you're only allowed?
KERRY: I couldn't go there no other time.
MARLENE: Couldn't?
KERRY: Are ya deaf, ya bloody deaf dora?
MARLENE: Well, what do ya mean ya couldn't?
KERRY: I couldn't go into the cemetery when there was whitefellas there.
MARLENE: Says who?
KERRY: Just the rules. Always been. I dunno.
MARLENE: Ya can't go to the cemetery and look at dead people except on a Sunday?
KERRY: We can go to the cemetery on a Sund'y and to the laundromat on a Frid'y. We're allowed into the pictures and we line up with everyone else but we can only sit down the front and we have to leave just before the picture is finished. We're not allowed into any government buildings in town, neither.
MARLENE: Why you tellin' me this stuff?
KERRY: Well. You're the same.
MARLENE: No way, not me.
KERRY: Yeah.
MARLENE: You callin' me a boong?
KERRY: Nah.
MARLENE: Yeah, ya are.
KERRY: If the cap fits.
MARLENE: Well, it doesn't fit, al'rite?

Pause.

KERRY: Soon tell.
MARLENE: What?
KERRY: When ya come of age you'll know.
MARLENE: How do ya figure that?
KERRY: Boongs can't vote.
MARLENE: What's that?
KERRY: Like, for the government.
MARLENE: That's not true.
KERRY: Yeah. We part of the flora and fauna, girl.
MARLENE: Don't say we.
KERRY: Okay.

MARLENE: 'Cause I'm not a boong.

KERRY: How come?

MARLENE: Boongs are drunks and they don't work and they're real dirty.

KERRY: How do you know so much about them, then?

MARLENE: Everyone knows that.

KERRY: So what are you?

MARLENE: My dad. He's different.

KERRY: But he's black.

MARLENE: But he's a good one. There are lots of good ones. Not all blacks are boongs.

Pause. KERRY *nods, knowingly.*

KERRY: Yeah, but all boongs are black, sister.

MARLENE *becomes her older self.*

MARLENE: They came and arrested us and they charged us. They charged us with neglect and they put us in the cells. For a week. We was all together but we were in a gaol cell. Why did they do that? They should have put us with Aunty. Or put us with another family.

Me and Christina were in Bidura and the boys were in the place down the road from there. The boys home. And we used to all go to the pictures on a Saturday and we'd see them at the Valhalla and then one day they weren't there. I sang out to the other boys where's my brothers and they said they've been transferred to another home. After that I just watched Christina all the time and I'd go to the baby's room, 'cause she was in a different room, and make sure she was all right, and I'd have to go to school and I didn't want to go to school because I didn't want to leave her in case she disappeared. And then one day she disappeared. [*Beat.*] I did watch her. I couldn't stop them.

♦ ♦ ♦ ♦ ♦

SCENE FOUR

The girls line up for a dormitory inspection. They show their sheets and their underpants.

MARLENE: What's happening?
MAREE: Dormitory check. You know the drill.
MARLENE: What would happen if they found something?
JUDI: Straight to solitary.
MAREE: Which is a mattress. No bed.
KERRY: Barefoot, lights on all the time, bread and water.
JUDI: Or they'd probably make all of us 'stand out'.
MAREE: Perfectly still.
KERRY: For hours.
MAREE: How about that time I spoke in the dorm and had to stand still for five days?
JUDI: Yeah, but you got rocks in your head, so it's easier for you.

Two women tuck MELANIE *into bed. The others exit.*

CORAL enters and walks toward where MELANIE is sleeping. She gently shakes her.

CORAL: Melanie. Psst. Melanie.
MELANIE: What?
CORAL: You were snoring.
MELANIE: Was not.
CORAL: Yeah. And you was crying in your sleep.
MELANIE: Shut up, Coral.
CORAL: Were so.
MELANIE: Shut up or I'll bash ya.
CORAL: Yeah, go on.
MELANIE: What? You want me to bash you, do you?
CORAL: I'm not scared of you.
MELANIE: Go back to sleep, Coral.

Pause.

CORAL: I'm gonna tell the Super.
MELANIE: Go on, then.
CORAL: I will. I could.

MELANIE: Tell him what?
CORAL: Tell him what that guard did to you.
MELANIE: [*sitting up*] What guard?
CORAL: Down in the showers.
MELANIE: What?
CORAL: I saw him. I saw what he did to you.
MELANIE: What are you talking about, Coral?
CORAL: He did it to you and then he told you that you were a good girl.

Pause.

MELANIE: Keep your voice down.
CORAL: I'm gonna tell the Super.
MELANIE: Are you?
CORAL: Yep.
MELANIE: That he did that to me?
CORAL: Yep.

Pause.

MELANIE: That won't get him into trouble, you know.
CORAL: Yes it will.
MELANIE: No. It will get me into trouble. For being a liar.
CORAL: But I saw him do it.
MELANIE: So it will get you and me into trouble.
CORAL: And him.
MELANIE: No. Not him.
CORAL: It will.
MELANIE: No.
CORAL: It will. It will. It has to.

Pause.

MELANIE: Go back to sleep.
CORAL: I'm gonna tell them. Tomorrow.
MELANIE: They'll find out.
CORAL: No they won't.
MELANIE: They'll examine me.
CORAL: Who will?
MELANIE: Doctor Fingers.

Pause.

CORAL: So?

MELANIE: Then they'll examine you. And they'll know that you're talking about yourself.

Pause.

CORAL: Well, what am I gonna say?
MELANIE: Nothing.
CORAL: I can't say nothing.
MELANIE: Why not?

Pause.

CORAL: I think there's something wrong.
MELANIE: Like what?
CORAL: My blood's stopped.
MELANIE: Shit.
CORAL: I have to stick something up there. Or tell him.
MELANIE: Don't tell him.
CORAL: Maybe he'll help me.
MELANIE: Shhh! You'll have to say you were already gone when you came in here.
CORAL: But Doctor Fingers examined me.
MELANIE: They won't care about that. If you say you were already gone they'll say they made a mistake.
CORAL: But why would they?
MELANIE: Because it will make it easier for them.
CORAL: Can't you stick something up there?
MELANIE: No.
CORAL: Please?
MELANIE: Go back to sleep, Coral.
CORAL: I can't. [*Beat.*] Can I climb in with you?
MELANIE: No.
CORAL: Please.
MELANIE: No. Now shut up.

Pause.

CORAL: He told me I was a good girl.
MELANIE: I bet he did.
CORAL: A good girl.
MELANIE: Yeah.

CORAL *exits.* MELANIE *goes back to sleep.*

LYNETTE *is still sitting outside. She steps forward, rubbing a spot near her clavicle.*

LYNETTE: Even though I've been told that I am the bastard scum of the earth, I love and accept myself completely.

Throughout the first half of the following she taps her forehead, under her eye, under her mouth, on the sides of her fingers.

Even though I been told I am incapable of trust, I love and accept myself completely. Even though I been told I'd be unable to maintain a relationship, I love and accept myself completely. Even though I have immense problems with parenting, I love and accept myself completely. Even though I been told that I am worth nothing, I love and accept myself completely. Even though I been told that I would end up in the gutter, I love and accept myself completely. Even though I been told that no one wanted me or ever would, I love and accept myself completely. Even though I been told I'll never be any good, that I'm useless, I'm pathetic and I'm a sook… I love and accept myself completely. And I am capable of going inside my former place of detention. I am going inside my former place of detention. I will soon go inside.

She finishes the routine and sits down, unable to go inside.

SCENE FIVE

The dining room. All the cast march in, in formation, and sit at a long table, to eat their meal.

JUDI: Do the impersonation again.
MAREE: You vill eat your vrankvort!
MARLENE: It's Matron.
MAREE: You vill eat your vrankvort and your spinach or I vill send you back to Hungary!
KERRY: Back to where?
MAREE: Back to Hungary. Where I am from.
MARLENE: Hey, you're good, Maree. Isn't she good, Melanie?
MELANIE: She's all right.

MAREE: All right? All right! For zat you vill get no weevils in your porridge in ze morning. And you vill have no lumps in your mashed potatoes. You vill not be getting everyzing zat ze other girls vill be lucky enough to be getting.
MELANIE: And she's not from Hungary, she's from Russia.
JUDI: She is not. She's from Germany.
MAREE: I am from Hungary. Hungary. Otherwise how could I so happily let you go hungary?
KERRY: Yeah, she does that often enough.
MAREE: Silence. Silence. Ve know zat you are only like zis because you vant ze part in ze Shakespeare play for yourself.
MELANIE: Shut up, Maree.
MAREE: It is true! But ze only vay you are going to get it is to be eating ze big balls. Ze big meatballs vith big chunks of ze onion.
CORAL: Yack. Cack. Poo.

From left: Annie Byron as Gayle, Lisa Flanagan as Kerry, Leah Purcell as Marlene, Carole Skinner as Judi, Jeanette Cronin as Melanie and Genevieve Hegney (behind) as Maree in the 2007 Company B production in Sydney. (Photo: Heidrun Löhr)

MAREE: Don't you be saying ze poo, you. You. Don't you be saying ze poo. Not all ze food is horrible to you because I can see she is putting on ze vreight. Eh, you girl. You are packing on ze vreight.
MELANIE: Stop it now, Maree.
MAREE: Yack, cack, poo, you say to ze meatballs. Ze lovely big meatballs zat hang from ze vaist of ze Zuperintendent.
GAYLE: Not the waist. Keep going, Matron.
MAREE: I love to suck ze balls of ze Zuperintendent. And he loves to suck mine!

The girls are all laughing ridiculously.

MARLENE: If you vill not eat ze rissoles, zen you vill have to eat ze rhubarb.

All the girls ooh and ah.

MELANIE: Marlene. Don't you start.
MARLENE: Ze rhubarb is lovely vith ze snotty, yellow custard.
MELANIE: I told you to shut up.
MARLENE: Come on, Coral, come here now and eat ze rhubarb vith lovely, long, yellow pieces of snot.

CORAL *breaks free from the table and goes and throws up in the corner.*

MAREE: What's wrong with her?
MELANIE: I told you to shut your mouth.
KERRY: Why would she throw up?
MARLENE: What's going on, Melanie?
MELANIE: Leave her alone. I told you.
MAREE: She'll have to go to Dorm Four.
MARLENE: What's Dorm Four?
MELANIE: It's where you go if you're unwell.
KERRY: Or up the duff.
MARLENE: What's that?
MAREE: That's what happens when the boogey man comes and gets you in the night.
MARLENE: The what?
MELANIE: The boogey man.

Pause.

MAREE: Has the boogey man ever come and got you, Melanie?

MELANIE: No.
MAREE: Then how come you know about it?
MELANIE: I dunno. Stories. Stuff other girls talk about in here.
MAREE: In the night.
MELANIE: Yeah.
GAYLE: In your own house?
MELANIE: Yeah, I guess so.
MAREE: So it has to be someone who lives with you. [*Pause.*] Like your brother maybe.
MELANIE: As if your brother would do that? Is that what your brother did?
MAREE: No. I don't have a deviant brother.
MELANIE: Well, neither do I.
GAYLE: So it must be your father, then.

    Pause.

MELANIE: What?
GAYLE: I've heard girls say their father did stuff to them.
MELANIE: What girls?
GAYLE: I dunno. Girls who were in here.
MELANIE: What girls?
GAYLE: I don't know.
MELANIE: Shut up, it's Matron.

♦ ♦ ♦ ♦ ♦

SCENE SIX

The girls put on small hats, as if they are in a chapel, and begin to sing a hymn.

ALL: [*singing*] Christ the Lord is risen today, Alleluia!
    Earth and heaven in chorus say, Alleluia!
    Raise your joys and triumphs high, Alleluia!
    Sing, ye heavens, and earth reply, Alleluia!
    They all kneel down, except for GAYLE.

KERRY: What are you doing?
GAYLE: It's all right.

KERRY: Gayle. You have to get on your knees.
GAYLE: No. I don't believe in kneeling so I'll just explain. He'll listen to me because I'm House Captain.
KERRY: Well, you'd better because he's coming over.
ALL: [*singing*] Love's redeeming work is done, Alleluia!
    Fought the fight, the battle won, Alleluia!
    Death in vain forbids Him rise, Alleluia!
    Christ has opened paradise, Alleluia!
GAYLE: I'd like to choose not to kneel, sir.
KERRY: Gayle, just do it.
GAYLE: No, I'm not being disrespectful but, you see, I don't believe in God and so it would be more disrespectful to pretend I did.
ALL: [*singing*] Lives again our glorious King, Alleluia!
    Where, O death, is now thy sting? Alleluia!
    Once He died our souls to save, Alleluia!
    Where's thy victory, boasting grave? Alleluia!
GAYLE: It was a priest, sir, he hurt me when I was thirteen and ever since then I haven't believed in God. [*Pause.*] I'd really rather not disrespect God by kneeling, sir.

    GAYLE *is forced down onto the ground. She reacts as if she is taking blow after blow to the head and legs and arms and back.*

ALL: [*singing*] Soar we now where Christ has led, Alleluia!
    Following our exalted Head, Alleluia!
    Made like Him, like Him we rise, Alleluia!
    Ours the cross, the grave, the skies, Alleluia!
GAYLE: [*screaming*] Stop it. Stop it.
ALL: [*singing*] Hail the Lord of earth and heaven, Alleluia!
    Praise to Thee by both be given, Alleluia!
    Thee we greet triumphant now, Alleluia!
    Hail the Resurrection, Thou, Alleluia!

    CORAL *suddenly stands up.*

MELANIE: Coral, get down or you'll get the same.

    But CORAL *remains standing.*

CORAL: I told him.
MELANIE: You did what?
CORAL: I had to.

MELANIE: No, not like this, Coral.
CORAL: No, sir, I believe in God. But I don't think Gayle should be forced to kneel.

>CORAL *reacts as she is 'hit' in the face and the stomach.* MELANIE *watches her and then she stands.*

MELANIE: Neither do I, sir.
MARLENE: Or me.
MELANIE: Marlene, get back down.
MARLENE: If you're standing, I'm standing.

> CORAL *mimes taking repeated blows to the stomach.*

MELANIE: When he gets to you, don't cry.
MARLENE: What?
MELANIE: Whatever you do, don't cry. Don't give him the satisfaction.
MARLENE: Yep, don't cry.
MELANIE: And look him in the eye when he comes up to you. Like you're not scared of him.
MARLENE: Don't cry. Look him in the eye.
MELANIE: Right.

> *Behind them the beating of* CORAL *continues. Then* MARLENE *is knocked to the ground and takes one kick and then* MELANIE *is knocked to the ground and reacts to the 'beating'.*

ALL: King of glory, soul of bliss, Alleluia!
Everlasting life is this, Alleluia!
Thee to know, Thy power to prove, Alleluia!
Thus to sing, and thus to love, Alleluia!

> *The lights change and the girls are sitting in a line, waiting.*

CORAL: He's busted my teeth.
MELANIE: Then why did you tell him?
MARLENE: Tell him what?
CORAL: Shut up, Melanie. Just shut up.
MELANIE: All right, all right. Are you all right?
CORAL: He kept kicking me.
MELANIE: In the stomach. I saw.
CORAL: Please, Melanie, please don't say anything.
MARLENE: Why was he kicking her in the stomach?

The other girls go into a huddle and begin to whisper.

MELANIE: And you, you can shut your mouth. You started this.
GAYLE: She didn't have to stand up. I was doing all right on my own.
MELANIE: Great. Fat lot of thanks that is.
GAYLE: I didn't ask for the little slut to help me.
MELANIE: You're the little slut.
MARLENE: Stop it. Stop it, both of you. Come on.

CORAL stands, with trepidation, and goes offstage.

Why was he kicking her in the stomach?
MELANIE: He was trying to kill the baby.
MARLENE: Why would he want to do that?
MELANIE: Why do you think?

MARLENE looks at her, realising.

♦ ♦ ♦ ♦ ♦

SCENE SEVEN

MAREE *enters, singing.*

MAREE: [*singing*] I have seen the lark soar high at morn,
    Heard his song up in the blue,
    I have heard the blackbird pipe his note,
    The thrush and the linnet too,
    But there's none of them can sing so sweet
    My singing bird as you.

    If I could lure my singing bird
    From his own cosy nest,
    If I could catch my singing bird
    I would warm him on my breast,
    For there's none of them can sing so sweet
    My singing bird as you.

GAYLE and KERRY enter, carrying a small soft toy.

GAYLE: Look what we found.

MAREE goes to snatch it, but GAYLE keeps it out of her hand.

What's this, then?
MAREE: Just some shit from Welfare.

GAYLE: You don't think it's shit, we found it in your bed.
MAREE: Only so that the officers wouldn't take it.
GAYLE: So Maree's a softie, is she?
MAREE: No way.
GAYLE: So prove it.
MAREE: What?
GAYLE: Rip its arm off.

Pause.

MAREE: Yeah. No problem.
GAYLE: Go on, then.

MAREE *tries to rip the arm.*

MAREE: It won't rip.
GAYLE: Musn't be doing it hard enough.
MAREE: Come on, Gayle. This is stupid. I don't like soft toys.
GAYLE: Rip it!

Pause. MAREE *yanks the arm of the toy and rips it.*

MAREE: There. Now do you believe me?

MAREE *rips the toy a bit more.*

GAYLE: Yeah. Righto. We just needed to make sure.

They exit. She clutches the teddy to her.

MAREE: Oh. Oh, I'm so sorry. I'm sorry. You'll be all right, I promise. I promise I'll get some cotton from the sewing room and I'll sew you up better than before. You're not angry at me, are you? Otherwise she would have done something even worse like make me burn you or something. Or make me throw you away. I'll never throw you away. I'll never never throw you away or let anyone find you or hurt you ever again. Shh. Mummy's here now. We'll sew you up as good as new.

♦ ♦ ♦ ♦ ♦

SCENE EIGHT

MAREE *ties a bedpan on her backside and walks 'outside'.*

LYNETTE: Maree?

MAREE: Yeah.
LYNETTE: Who's made you wear that?
MAREE: Who do you think?
LYNETTE: You can take it off now.
MAREE: Just have to put it back on again.
LYNETTE: What's it for?
MELANIE: It's for wetting the bed.
> *Pause.*

LYNETTE: What's wrong, Maree?
MAREE: Nothing.
LYNETTE: Come on. Take it off while you're out here with me.
> MAREE *looks around fearfully. Then she takes it off.*

You been wetting the bed again?
> MAREE *nods.*

MAREE: I try not to, Lynette, I try so hard not to. And now I'm not allowed to drink anything after lunch. Nothing at all so I don't wet the bed at night. But I get so thirsty.
> LYNETTE *pulls a little bottle out of her purse.*

LYNETTE: Here, have some of this.
MAREE: No.
LYNETTE: Go on.
MAREE: No. Then I'll wet the bed and it will be worse.
> *Pause.*

LYNETTE: What's happened, Maree?
MAREE: You know they told me that my family died in a car accident?
LYNETTE: Yeah.
MAREE: I found out that they're not really dead.
> *Pause.*

LYNETTE: But why would they tell you that they were?
MAREE: The Superintendent told me. You don't think my parents would have told him to say that?
LYNETTE: No. I think he was just being… I don't know why. I'll still never know why they'd do or say something like that.
> *Pause.*

MAREE: Swear to me that you won't tell.
LYNETTE: I swear. I swear I'll never tell a soul.
> MAREE *ties on the potty and exits.*
> LYNETTE *is crying when* JUDI *enters.*

JUDI: You all right out here?
LYNETTE: Just having a break.
> *Pause.*

JUDI: I found the schoolroom.
LYNETTE: Does it still have all the chairs set up?
JUDI: No, it still has the same smell, though.
LYNETTE: Chewing gum.
JUDI: Chalk dust.
LYNETTE: Tomato sauce.
JUDI: Round past the dining room.
LYNETTE: Thanks.
JUDI: You seen that? [*Pause.*] You've been in?
LYNETTE: Yeah. Well... no.
JUDI: Come on, then.
> LYNETTE *gets up. She is shaking with anticipation. Then she sits back down, crying.*

LYNETTE: I can't.
JUDI: Yeah. You can as soon as you stop that.
LYNETTE: I... what?
JUDI: You should stop that right now.
LYNETTE: But I thought... I thought we came here to...
JUDI: Not me.
> *Pause.* LYNETTE *dries her eyes a bit.*

LYNETTE: There's nothing wrong with crying.
JUDI: No one's doing anything to you now, are they?
LYNETTE: No.
JUDI: They're not shutting us in for the night, are they?
LYNETTE: No, but...
JUDI: But they did.
LYNETTE: Yes.
JUDI: And how many years ago was that? [*Pause.*] What do you think?

When you cry?
LYNETTE: What do you mean?
JUDI: I mean what do you think about to set the blubbering going?
LYNETTE: Just… looking at this place. The memories it holds.
JUDI: The bad memories.
LYNETTE: Yes.
JUDI: But the suffering here isn't your whole story, is it?
LYNETTE: No. But…
JUDI: No, but you get a certain thrill from dwelling on it.
LYNETTE: I do not.
JUDI: The cruelty of it. The horror of it.

Pause. CORAL *puts her head around the corner.*

CORAL: Oh. Don't let me intrude.
JUDI: Coral. Come here and tell us about that reunion.
CORAL: It was a great reunion, that one.
JUDI: Yeah, where'd you do that, then?
CORAL: Out at that Stonequarry Lodge at Picton.
JUDI: Oh, yeah.
CORAL: And we had a big feed at the Observer Hotel.
JUDI: So you said.
CORAL: Down in The Rocks.
JUDI: I haven't been there for years.
CORAL: Down in The Rocks.
JUDI: Nice it was, too?
CORAL: It was nice.
JUDI: Have a nice meal together?
CORAL: We booked in on that Captain Cook cruise.
JUDI: Harbour cruise?
CORAL: Didn't go.
JUDI: No?
CORAL: They told us to go to the back of the line, didn't they?
JUDI: Who told you?
CORAL: That tour lady.
JUDI: She didn't.
CORAL: We was all lined up at the front.
JUDI: Yeah.
CORAL: And then the boat came.

JUDI: Yeah.
CORAL: And she said, you know, 'Could you ladies wait at the back while we board the other passengers.'
JUDI: That was queer.
CORAL: Wasn't it, though?
JUDI: And you were all the Parramatta Girls?
CORAL: All bein' told, you know, go to the back of the queue.
JUDI: No.
CORAL: Go to the bottom of the pile.
JUDI: No.
CORAL: You know.
JUDI: But why did she say that?
CORAL: I dunno, but she musta thought she'd unboxed a bag of snakes.
JUDI: I can see yas.
CORAL: We were hissin' and carryin' on.
JUDI: I can see yas.
CORAL: Tellin' her what she could do with her Captain Cook cruise boat.
JUDI: Shove it.
CORAL: Sink it.
JUDI: Sink it!
CORAL: We was that furious.
JUDI: I know.
CORAL: That Parramatta. That spurted up.
JUDI: That old fire.
CORAL: Like a volcano.
JUDI: Yeah?
CORAL: You know.
JUDI: Oh, I do know.
CORAL: Just spurted up.
JUDI: And you didn't go?
CORAL: Booked the cruise.
JUDI: Booked it in.
CORAL: Thirty women.
JUDI: All dressed up.
CORAL: Didn't go.
JUDI: No.

CORAL: Wouldn't go to the back of the line.
JUDI: Why would you?
CORAL: You know.
JUDI: Just saw red.
LYNETTE: 'Go to the back of the queue.'
JUDI: So wrong.
CORAL: We were just standin' there.
JUDI: Waitin'.
CORAL: The boat comes in and there she is, all in her Captain Cook uniform.
JUDI: 'Go to the back of the queue.'
CORAL: I wasn't 'avin' it.
LYNETTE: Why would you?
CORAL: And then all the other ladies wouldn't go neither.
JUDI: They're good girls.
CORAL: My feet were aching.
JUDI: They're not young anymore.
CORAL: Standin', waitin' for the boat.
LYNETTE: 'Go to the back of the queue.'
CORAL: Eh? What's that about?
JUDI: Did ya get your money back?
CORAL: Oh, they had to give us a refund.
JUDI: Too right.
CORAL: And apologise.
JUDI: Fancy.
CORAL: And we still wouldn't get on the boat.

> JUDI *laughs.*

And the Captain Cook girl, she wished she'd never seen the likes of us.
ALL: 'Go to the back of the queue.'
CORAL: She won't be sayin' that again for a while.
JUDI: No chance.
CORAL: Can't force me to do something I don't want to.
JUDI: No.

> *Behind them,* LYNETTE *stands and goes into the home.* CORAL *and* JUDI *follow her, thrilled.*

♦♦♦♦♦

SCENE NINE

MARLENE *walks past them, carrying a big pot of stew.*

She notices that the back gate is open. She looks around and goes to call someone, but panics when she realises she's holding the pot of stew.

She puts the pot down and runs back and forth across the stage, wondering what she should do.

She runs back to the side of the stage where she meets KERRY.

MARLENE *can't speak. She is shaking her head.*

KERRY: What?
MARLENE: I couldn't go. Even though it was right there.
KERRY: Couldn't go where? Where's the stew?
MARLENE: I put it down.
KERRY: You what?
MARLENE: I put it down.
KERRY: You did what?
MARLENE: I put it down.
KERRY: Bloody hell. They're going to kill us. That's the stew.
MARLENE: I know.
KERRY: So where'd you put it down?
MARLENE: On the way. On the way to the girls in isolation.
KERRY: You were supposed to take the girls in isolation their stew.
MARLENE: I know. And then I couldn't.
KERRY: Why not?
MARLENE: I don't know.
KERRY: Why not, Marlene?
MARLENE: I was scared.
KERRY: Scared of what?
MARLENE: Come and look.

They run to centre stage and KERRY *sees the open gate.*

KERRY: Bloody hell. They've left the gate open.
MARLENE: Who did?

KERRY: I dunno. The garbage men, probably. Come on.
MARLENE: What?
KERRY: Come on, let's go.
MARLENE: Go where?
KERRY: Escape. You coming?
MARLENE: I can't.
KERRY: Why not?
MARLENE: I just can't.
KERRY: Come on, Marlene, I'll look after you. [*Pause.*] Come on or I'll go without you.

> MARLENE *remains frozen.* KERRY *gives her a goodbye hug, then exits towards the gate.* MARLENE *picks up the pot of stew. She looks out, wistfully.*
>
> *The lights fade.*

END OF ACT ONE

ACT TWO

SCENE ONE

KERRY *and* CORAL *enter as older women.*

KERRY: Hey, Coral.
CORAL: Hey, Kerry.
KERRY: Do ya reckon you got treated different in here?
CORAL: Oh, for sure.
KERRY: Do ya?
CORAL: Yeah. Well, it's obvious, isn't it? [*Pause.*] Me arms.
KERRY: What about yer arms?
CORAL: They're shorter than most people's.
KERRY: Are they?
CORAL: Yeah, they're only just beyond what you'd call stumps.
KERRY: Is that why you always wear long sleeves?
CORAL: Yeah. Because that's a sign of the bad blood.

They compare the length of their arms.

KERRY: Your arms are as long as mine.
CORAL: As short, ya mean. Which goes to prove my point. Short arms. Bad blood.
KERRY: What exactly is bad blood?
CORAL: Freckles are another sign.
KERRY: You don't have freckles.
CORAL: If your eyes are closer together, if you can't roll up the sides of your tongue, freckles, short arms and the most obvious of all…
KERRY: What?
CORAL: Like both of us…
KERRY: What?
CORAL: PB. Pointy boobs. The pointier they are the badder you turned out.

KERRY looks at her and then laughs.

KERRY: Ya bloody nutter. It is not.

CORAL: Yeah, but that's what they used to believe. That they could know you was a crim by looking at your face and measuring your forehead.

KERRY: Yeah. [*Beat.*] Seriously, ya reckon us blackfellas had it tougher in here?

CORAL: I don't reckon there was black and white in here.

KERRY: Just black and blue, eh?

They exit.

MELANIE *and the other girls are hanging sheets on the clothes line.*

ALL: [*singing*] The water is wide, I cannot get o'er,
Neither have I the wings to fly,
Give me a boat that can carry two,
And both shall row, my love and I.

A ship there is and she sails the sea,
She's loaded deep as deep can be,
But not so deep as the love I'm in,
I know not if I sink or swim.

I leaned my back against an oak
Thinking it was a trusty tree,
But first it bent and then it broke,
So did my love prove false to me.

Oh, love be handsome, love be bold,
Bright as a jewel when first it is new,
But love grows old and waxes cold
And fades away like the morning dew.

They proceed to do laundering things with the sheets.

MAREE: They're saying someone has escaped.

MELANIE: That's right.

MAREE: It's Coral, isn't it?

MELANIE: What?

MAREE: She wasn't in her bed last night.

MELANIE *puts down what she's doing and holds* MAREE *by the shoulders.*

MELANIE: What?

The girls stop singing.

MAREE: Coral's gone. So she must be the one who escaped.

    MAREE *exits.*

MARLENE: It was Kerry who escaped out the gate. So where's Coral?

MELANIE: They must have taken her to the hospital.

MARLENE: To have the baby?

MELANIE: That'll be the end of her sentence.

MARLENE: We have to get her to send a photo.

MELANIE: Of what?

MARLENE: Of bubs.

MELANIE: She won't get to keep it.

    Pause.

MARLENE: What?

MELANIE: They take them.

MARLENE: No, they can't do that.

    MELANIE *throws her a 'yeah right' look and exits.* GAYLE *enters. Her left arm is bandaged. When she sees* MARLENE *she hides it behind her back.*

Hey, aren't you supposed to be in the laundry?

GAYLE: I've been helping the doctor.

MARLENE: What's behind your back?

GAYLE: Nothing. Get lost.

MARLENE: Show us.

    They struggle. MARLENE *sees that* GAYLE *has a bandaged arm.*

So what's that from?

GAYLE: The doctor was taking a skin graft.

MARLENE: What for?

GAYLE: Um… He says I've got exceptionally smooth skin.

MARLENE: So?

GAYLE: So, Lux are looking for… models.

MARLENE: For what?

GAYLE: For their soap ads. Like, you know how you have all these women doing ads about how gentle Lux is on your skin? Well, they reckon I've got really smooth skin and it's so good I could maybe be in a Lux commercial.

MARLENE: You are so full of shit, Gayle Ford.
GAYLE: No, just in the background. Not in the front of the picture, you know, not where the star is, but in the back.

Pause.

MARLENE: [*looking at the bandage*] Isn't that where your tatt is?
GAYLE: Well, that's why they have to get rid of it. So I can be in the ad.
MARLENE: You can't get rid of a tattoo. It's right in your skin.
GAYLE: Yeah, well, they did.

GAYLE unwraps part of the bandage. Her arm is a bloody mess.

MARLENE: Looks bad.
GAYLE: Yeah, well, it has to look like that at first. But it will heal.
MARLENE: What did he do it with?
GAYLE: I did it.
MARLENE: With what?
GAYLE: With a bowl of warm water and salt and… steel wool.
MARLENE: You shouldn't have done that.
GAYLE: No. The doctor showed me. It's not normal steel wool that you use in the kitchen. This is surgical steel wool.
MARLENE: Did it hurt?

GAYLE, who has been keeping it together, bites her lip to stop herself from crying. She nods.

GAYLE: A bit. But it will heal. Don't you reckon?
MARLENE: Oh, yeah. It will heal. I'm sure it will.
GAYLE: It looks bad, it looks really bad, but he's a doctor, right? From England even. He must know.
MARLENE: Of course he would.
GAYLE: And then no tattoo.
MARLENE: And then you can be in the Lux soap commercial.
GAYLE: Just up the back.
MARLENE: Yeah. Just up the back.

◆ ◆ ◆ ◆ ◆

SCENE TWO

MAREE *and* LYNETTE *are folding sheets when* JUDI *comes in. She pulls out a cigarette.*

LYNETTE: Wow! Where'd you get that?

JUDI gives it to LYNETTE *and takes out another.*

MAREE: Bloody hell! Are you some kind of magician?

She gives it to MAREE *and then pulls out yet another.*

LYNETTE: Judi, what are you doing?

JUDI: Plenty more where that came from.

She pulls out an entire packet.

MAREE: What did you do? Raid the officers' lockers?

JUDI: Nah. Stephenson gave them to me.

Pause.

LYNETTE: Why would he do that?

JUDI: I touched his thing.

MAREE: Really?

JUDI: Yeah.

LYNETTE: When?

JUDI: I was cleaning up his office, right? And he told me to dust the shelves. And the next thing I turn around and he's got it out and he's touching it. Right? And so I think, shit.

MAREE: Because he always looks at you funny.

LYNETTE: He used to look at Coral but lately he's been looking at you.

JUDI: Coral was a sap.

MAREE: What?

JUDI: So he's standing there with this… thing in his hand right.

LYNETTE: How big was it?

JUDI: Two pebbles and a twig.

LYNETTE *laughs.*

MAREE: And so what did you do?

JUDI: He just stood there, right? And I'm looking at him and at… it. And then I just went over and touched it and he gave me this packet of cigarettes.

MAREE: You gotta be more careful, Judi.

JUDI: It's fine. He just rubbed his hand on it and held my hand on it and then after a couple of minutes it went down again.

LYNETTE: A whole packet!

MAREE: He won't let it go now, you know.

Valerie Bader (left) as Lynette and Carole Skinner as Judi in the 2007 Company B production in Sydney. (Photo: Heidrun Löhr)

JUDI: Good. Next time he can give me something else.
LYNETTE: What? Would you do it with him?
JUDI: No way. But if it's just my hand.
MAREE: He'll want you to put it in your mouth.
JUDI: Yeah, well if he does he can get me outta here on a Sunday afternoon. Like when he takes those other girls on excursions.
MAREE: You don't know what you're doing.
JUDI: Yeah. I do. And he'll have to let me play Portia in the play. When the ABC come to record.
MAREE: Stupid little bitch.
JUDI: What?
MAREE: I know what they can do.
JUDI: You do not.
MAREE: I've had a baby.
LYNETTE: Since when?
MAREE: A year ago.
LYNETTE: Where's it now?
MAREE: [*with a shrug*] Adopted, somewhere.
LYNETTE: Didn't you want to keep it?
MAREE: [*with a shrug*] Nah.

Pause.

JUDI: Well, I'm not letting him put it in me, so I won't get pregnant, will I?
MAREE: You won't be able to stop him.
JUDI: Well then, he would have done it anyway, wouldn't he? At least this way I get something out of it.

MAREE *exits.* LYNETTE *remains with* JUDI. JUDI *tips all the cigarettes out of the packet and counts them.*

It's like they can't hear the words comin' out of your mouth. That's why they need you to smile all the time.
LYNETTE: Who?
JUDI: The officers. They're like dogs, they respond to the tone of your voice, to the attitude of how you're standing. They don't actually hear words, they just see and sense your mood, and if you're not sweet, you know ya gotta be obedient.
LYNETTE: Obedient?
JUDI: Yeah. [*She pants like a dog.*] So you can't talk to them. Ya have to

appeal to them, ya have to bring something out in them.
LYNETTE: How?
JUDI: You can't be obvious. Like you can't just wink, you know. Ya gotta flaunt it.
LYNETTE: Flaunt what?
JUDI: Your... appeal.
LYNETTE: I don't have any appeal. I don't have anything to flaunt.
JUDI: Ya do.
LYNETTE: I don't. And anyway, why should I?
JUDI: You wanna be drugged. With Largactyl?
LYNETTE: They can't drug you.
JUDI: Wake up, slag. Wake up. You're in here. They can do whatever they want to you. Whatever they want.
LYNETTE: But I don't have anything. I don't have anything they want.
JUDI: You've gotta find something.

♦ ♦ ♦ ♦ ♦

SCENE THREE

GAYLE *is in isolation. The bandages are still on her arms. She unwraps them and her arms are a scarred and bloody mess. She begins to rub herself on the walls of the isolation cell.*

GAYLE: A scab carries away all the old skin. Carries away all the old skin. Carries away all the old.

She continues to rub herself on the bricks of the walls of the isolation cell. Her arms and legs are covered in blood, and blood runs down her forehead.

♦ ♦ ♦ ♦ ♦

SCENE FOUR

LYNETTE *and* JUDI *appear as older women.* LYNETTE *is a bit distracted by her own experience of being inside the home, staring as* GAYLE *continues rubbing.*

JUDI: Do you wanna hear a funny story? About numbers.

LYNETTE: What numbers?

JUDI: Eighteen-and-a-half to twenty-four. That's when I worked in the brothels. And five. That's how many terminations I've had.

LYNETTE: Right.

JUDI: I carried one baby full term, but it was stillborn. Which was a shame because I was going to keep her. Probably just as well for her that I didn't.

LYNETTE: I'm sure that's not true.

JUDI: After that, I cut myself off from the scene. I just wanted to get on with my life and have a baby and be looked after.

LYNETTE: That'd be nice.

JUDI: By now I was twenty-five. Got married, tried everything to get pregnant. Tubes were blocked. So I said, can we adopt? No way, he said. But then he changed his mind. So we got the papers and you fill 'em out and you send them off. And I remember down the bottom it said, any criminal records, and if so what are they? I just put yes. So the chap came out and he's sitting in the lounge. And he had the papers and he was only a young bloke and he looked really embarrassed and he said, 'Ah, you've put down you've got some criminal records and we looked it up,' and he says, 'Do you know there's a number of them?' So I said, 'What number?' And he said, 'Six hundred. There's more than six hundred charges.'

LYNETTE: And what did you say?

JUDI: I said, 'Really, that's terrible.' So I said, 'But I haven't had any for six years, you know.' So this guy says, 'If you still want to adopt, you're going to have to get people who knew you then and know you now, to speak up on your behalf.' So I did. Cops. And we brought her home in September. Third of the ninth, 1972. And that was the loveliest number of them all. [*Pause.*] I would have liked to see some of the old girls. Just to see how many of them came up with the same numbers.

LYNETTE: And have you seen anyone?

    Pause.

JUDI: Yes.

LYNETTE: Who?

JUDI: Someone who recognised me. Who remembered what I'd done with the Superintendent. Being his favourite.

LYNETTE: And what did you do?
JUDI: I told her she was mistaken.
> *Pause.*

LYNETTE: You have to talk to her.
JUDI: No. I really can't, Lynette. I really can't.
LYNETTE: You have to.
JUDI: I don't and I won't.
> JUDI *exits.*

♦♦♦♦♦

SCENE FIVE

MELANIE: After they took Coral away, I guess I sort of jumped the rails. I made up these drinks, sorta cocktails, out of Brasso and some other stuff, and got all these girls to drink it. Sort of made us dizzy and that. But when it came to punish us they only had six isolation cells so they got us to do a loft job. That was above the laundry, the loft. [*Looking around*] Imagine this without the walls, just the beams. And the roof, with no roofing on it, just the beams. And all these pigeons and pigeon shit everywhere, right, and a wooden floor. You had your breakfast and then you went up there at seven o'clock in the morning.
> MAREE *enters.*

MAREE: Stand.
> KERRY *stands in front of a wooden beam.*

Dip your brush.
> *The girls dip their brushes.*

Scrub.
> *The girls all scrub. They scrub and scrub.*

MELANIE: You would scrub in this position for half and hour. And it'd be a beam that was this far in front of you. You weren't allowed to brush the shit off your hands. If she said dip your brush, you just had to let all the shit run down your arms for half an hour while you scrubbed. I didn't mind. Because I deserved it. I was a bad girl and

I deserved it. I'd wished my father dead, see, and soon after that he got sick. Really sick. And because everyone in Parramatta told me I was bad. One day Matron said to me, 'Well, it's no wonder, really, a daughter like you. You'd drive anyone to an early grave.' And I bought it. I was bad, powerfully bad, and I needed to be punished. And the more violent I was, the worse I was punished. Which is what I wanted. Because I had to create the kind of badness that might be able to make someone sick just by hating them enough. Children. You tell them they're animals, you treat them like animals. And they become.

MARLENE enters and sees KERRY is back.

MAREE: Stop.

KERRY stops scrubbing.

Brush down.

KERRY puts her brush down.

Half an hour.

MAREE exits. MARLENE throws her arms around KERRY.

MARLENE: Kerry!

KERRY: Hello, Marlene.

KERRY is a shadow of her former self. Really flat and quiet and broken.

MARLENE: What are you doing back?

KERRY: Caught me.

MARLENE: Where'd you go?

KERRY: Cross.

MARLENE: Yeah?

KERRY: Hung out with Lizzie and Kay. Only Kay's an albino.

MARLENE: A what?

KERRY: Albino. Pure white. White hair, white eyes.

MARLENE: Ya coulda picked someone a bit less conspicuous.

KERRY: Yeah, that's what the cops said.

Pause.

MARLENE: How'd you get to the Cross?

KERRY: Hitched.

MARLENE: So now what?

KERRY: Original nine months, plus another nine months for the escape.
MARLENE: Reckon they'll want you back in the kitchen.

    KERRY *just sits rocking, broken.*

Kerry? [*Pause.*] Kerry?

    MAREE *enters and overhears* MARLENE.

MAREE: Leave her.
MARLENE: What?
MAREE: I said, leave her.
MARLENE: What's wrong with her?
MAREE: She's been given a good going-over.

    KERRY *looks at* MARLENE. *Her eyes are like a wounded animal.*

Stand.

    The girls stand.

Dip your brush.

    The girls dip their brushes.

Scrub.

    The girls scrub. MARLENE *looks at* KERRY *but* KERRY *is scrubbing with a vacant stare.*

◆ ◆ ◆ ◆ ◆

SCENE SIX

MARLENE, *trapped in a living nightmare, is surrounded by girls dressed in sheets. They run around her, except for* KERRY *who remains small and shattered on her seat.*

KERRY: Come on, I'll look after you.
GAYLE: It was surgical steel wool.
JUDI: The court will come to order.
MARLENE: They can't do that.
MELANIE: She won't get to keep it.
MAREE: She's been given a good going-over.
MARLENE: If I behave myself.
KERRY: Nine months.
MELANIE: They take them.

KERRY: Plus another nine months for the escape.
CORAL: He's busted my teeth.
MARLENE: They can't do that.
MELANIE: That's what happens when the boogey man comes and gets you in the night.
JUDI: Silence in the court.
MARLENE: This place doesn't scare me.
MELANIE: Don't cry.
GAYLE: Look him in the eye.
CORAL: He kept kicking me.
MAREE: She'll have to go to Dorm Four.
JUDI: You wanna be drugged with Largactyl?
KERRY: Come on, or I'll go without you.

The girls throw the sheets at MARLENE. MARLENE *screams uncontrollably, all the loss and pain and grief and anger coming out in one massive raging scream of fury and humiliation and frustration. Then she runs off.*

♦ ♦ ♦ ♦ ♦

SCENE SEVEN

MAREE *enters. She closes a door and stands with her back pressed against it. She gets a chair and jams the door shut. Then she takes a small rope out of her pocket and looks at it. She begins to hum the tune of 'The Singing Bird'.*

On the other side of the stage, MELANIE *enters and sits down. She takes a sharp object and cuts herself with it.*

MARLENE *gets up from the corner and goes over to* MELANIE. *They look at each other.*

MELANIE: Have you cut yourself before?
MARLENE: Not really.
MELANIE: You can't go too deep. Just enough for it to sting.

MELANIE *cuts down her leg. Blood begins to seep out of the wound.*

MARLENE: What does it feel like?

MELANIE: Just... like it releases the pressure or something.
MARLENE: Give it here.

> MARLENE *cuts down her arm.*

MELANIE: How's that?
MARLENE: Yeah. Good.

> *On the other side of the stage,* LYNETTE *is rattling the door knob. After some moments, there is a knock on the door.*

LYNETTE: Maree. [*She knocks again.*] Maree.

> MAREE *stuffs the rope back in her pocket.* LYNETTE *tries to open the door but it's jammed.*

MAREE: Yeah.
LYNETTE: Open the door.

> MAREE *moves the chair and opens the door.*

MAREE: What?
LYNETTE: You're not supposed to jam things against the door like that.
MAREE: I didn't. It was stuck.
LYNETTE: If I was Matron...
MAREE: So. What?
LYNETTE: Matron wants you to take the food to girls in the admissions room.
MAREE: Why me?
LYNETTE: Well, I didn't exactly ask, did I? Are you all right?
MAREE: I know why she wants me to do it.
LYNETTE: Why?
MAREE: She wants everyone to see me. That's why.

> MAREE *straps a white hospital bedpan onto the back of her pants and exits.*
>
> *On the other side of the stage,* MELANIE *cuts her leg again.*

MELANIE: I love it.
MARLENE: Why do you?
MELANIE: All the pain is just there. Just there on your leg, stinging. All there.
MARLENE: I do know.
MELANIE: I love seeing the blood come up, too. Like it always comes up. Like a little command. I cut and up comes the blood.

MARLENE: Like a little command, 'Come up blood'.
MELANIE: 'Front and centre blood.'
They are laughing.
You want to do one more?
MARLENE: Yeah.
MELANIE: A little bit deeper this time. Some real red, red blood. And it will really sting.
MARLENE takes the knife and is about to cut her arm again. She looks up at MELANIE. She throws the cutting implement away.
MARLENE: We can't let them win.
Pause.
MELANIE: That's what my dad always said.
MARLENE: Yeah, mine too.
MELANIE: I want to go home.
MARLENE: Then let's go home. See your dad.
MELANIE: He hurts me.
MARLENE: Does he?
MELANIE: He's great. And he's not. And I still want to go home.
MARLENE: Let's just get out of here.
MELANIE: How?
MARLENE: Escape.
Pause.
MELANIE: You didn't run out when the gate was open.
MARLENE: I know. So now I wanna.
MELANIE: Kerry tried.
MARLENE: Kerry hung around with an albino. We're smarter than that.
MELANIE: We can't escape. We're locked in.
MARLENE: Come on, let's try.
MELANIE stands where she is. MARLENE walks forward and becomes her older self.
We went around to the side, right past the school, and we were gonna try and climb over the wall there, over this big gate. But when we got there we realised we couldn't do that. We could hear everyone singin' out sayin', 'They're getting Jones,' and he really scared me.
MARLENE has been enacting her confusion and terror. She comes

to the side of the stage. She looks behind her, concerned, then climbs up a ladder onto the mezzanine.

So there was nowhere else to go except up on the roof and so we went onto the schoolhouse roof. And that was the first time anyone ever went on the roof. And when he came around... struttin' around... what's he gonna do? He's started yellin', 'Get off that roof or I'm gonna kill you... you pair of bastards, you wait 'til I get hold of you, Marlene... get down off that roof now.' And I said, 'No, fuck you'... and he went to climb up and that's when I thought, 'Oh, what are we gonna do?'

She pulls up one of the roof tiles and throws it down onto the stage. She continues throwing tiles (or paper files) onto the stage through the following speech.

I realised that you could pull the tiles up. So I pulled a tile off the roof and aimed it at his head and threw it at him. Because I really thought... I thought if he's gonna kill me... he's already said it... I'm gonna kill him first. And I threw the tile at him. Well, he scurried back down off the roof and he was standin' over there sayin', 'You come down, you little bitch,' and he was really wild. But he was too frightened to come back up. I just grabbed more tiles off then, and all the girls were all laughing because we pulled it off the roof. And they were all shoutin', 'Give it to him, give it to him.' And I pulled another one off and he was getting madder and madder but I knew he couldn't do anything. After about half an hour, and this went on, this screamin', and in the end he got one of the older girls to come around. She yelled up to us... 'He wants to make a deal if you come down, Marlene'... 'What will the deal be?' And I said, 'That he won't bash us. I know we have to go to isolation but he's not to bash us.' And she said, 'Okay, then that's what we'll make the deal... but come down because he doesn't want to have to call the fire brigade and he doesn't want to have to call the police.' So I said, 'Okay, but you're the witness to that he's said he won't bash us,' and I yelled that out. 'He's made a deal that he won't bash us but we're goin' to isolation.'

So by the time we got down all the girls were at the big tree where they all lined up because it was muster time and they're all lined up there. And we're walkin' around past 'em and Melanie was

Leah Purcell as Marlene in the 2007 Company B production in Sydney. (Photo: Heidrun Löhr)

that nervous that she nearly fell over, and I've always had a good sense of humour, so I just burst out laughin'... Well, he—an' I've got a loud laugh—he turned and run at me. He was gonna bash me then and there but all the girls turned around and Gayle yells out, 'Don't touch 'er,' and they all took a big step toward him and then he shit himself.

 He was scared. And, you know, when I remember this, that was the first time we'd been together. Looking back now, I can see it. He was actually scared of us. And er... he said, 'No I won't, come on then, I'm not gonna touch her,' and he stopped. See, he stopped what he was gonna do. He was gonna bash me but because she yelled out and they took a step toward him... he knew that they would attack... he did... and he said, 'Come on, you're getting into isolation,' and they put me in isolation and all the time I was in there I was thinkin' wasn't that fantastic... we really had it over him when we all stuck. What would happen if we all stuck like that all the time? The real hard thing was when we'd all stand there with each other and see the girl next to you knocked down and you can't help. You've got to stand there and watch that and wait for your turn. That used to get to me. 'Cause when I saw us turn that time and seen that we could be a force to be reckoned with, that's when I sort of got the idea I'm gonna talk to the girls about how we could get better conditions, and better clothes, and better food, and better facilities. You know, more blankets, we were only allowed one stupid cottony quilt and we were freezing. Hell, it was cold. We wanted blankets and we wanted to be treated not like animals. You know. These bashin's all the time. And so I said to the other girls, 'Why don't we riot?'

♦ ♦ ♦ ♦ ♦

SCENE EIGHT

The other girls whoop and woo-hoo as they enter. To the sound of smashing and crashing and banging, the riot plays out on stage. Paper files fly into the air.

There is, loudly, the sound of an ambulance siren.

MELANIE *enters with a long garden hose. She drags it across the stage, laughing.*

MARLENE: Now they're listening to us.
MELANIE: They sure are.
MARLENE: What's that for?

> MELANIE *begins to 'chop' the hose into tiny little bits with a small axe.*

MELANIE: This is what they can do with their hoses that they hose us down with.

> *She chops away. Behind them is the sound of a siren.*

And this is what they can do with their hoses that they cut up into bits and belt us with.

> KERRY *runs on.*

KERRY: Hey, there's an ambulance out the front. They're trying to open the gates.
MARLENE: What are they going to do to us?
MELANIE: They're not going to do anything.

> JUDI *runs on.*

JUDI: Did you see that they've called an ambulance?
MELANIE: Don't worry about it. It's just one more thing to try and freak us out.
MARLENE: They sure know how to do that.
JUDI: Well, what are we going to do now?
MELANIE: Marlene?
MARLENE: What?
MELANIE: What are we going to do now?

> *Pause.*

MARLENE: We're going to keep rioting until they close this place down.

> *All the girls whoop and woo-hoo.*

And if they won't close it down, we're gonna burn the little shithole down.

> *They continue to whoop and woo-hoo.* LYNETTE *runs on. She is agitated, urgent. The whooping stops as they notice her.*

LYNETTE: Quiet. Be quiet.
MARLENE: Lynette?

LYNETTE: You have to let the ambulance in the gate.
MARLENE: No way, that's just another way to get at us.
LYNETTE: [*screaming*] You have to let it in.
MELANIE: What is it, Lyn?
LYNETTE: Marlene, it's not for us.
MARLENE: Then who's it for?
MELANIE: Lynnie?
LYNETTE: It's Maree.
MARLENE: Where is Maree?
LYNETTE: I didn't know that she had a rope.

>   LYNETTE *shakes her head and runs off. They all exit after her.*

♦ ♦ ♦ ♦ ♦

SCENE NINE

CORAL *enters and begins to place upright the chairs that have been overturned in the riot.*

After a few moments GAYLE *enters. She helps with setting up the chairs for the speeches.*

CORAL: How you going?
GAYLE: Yeah, fine. It feels right to be here.
CORAL: Feel a bit like you've had a weight lifted off your shoulders.
GAYLE: Didn't even know I was carrying it.

>   *They both rotate their shoulders as if they're sore, and then laugh. Pause.*

CORAL: I couldn't help hearing.
GAYLE: What?
CORAL: When you were in the…
GAYLE: Where the doctor…
CORAL: Yeah. You said you had two lines on your file.
GAYLE: That's right.
CORAL: So you've read your file, then?
GAYLE: I have, yeah. Are you thinking of getting yours?
CORAL: Oh, I've got my file.
GAYLE: So you've read it?

CORAL: I haven't read it.
GAYLE: Oh. [*Beat.*] You've got it but you haven't read it?
> *Pause.* CORAL *reaches into her bag and pulls out a stack of photocopied pages.*

CORAL: They photocopied it for me.
GAYLE: God. They don't usually do that.
CORAL: I just told them they had to.
GAYLE: Usually you have to just go and look at it in a room with an officer of the Department present.
CORAL: I know. I just told them to copy it.
GAYLE: Good for you.
CORAL: And then I couldn't read it.
GAYLE: Well, the time will come.
CORAL: Yeah. That's right.
GAYLE: Just take your time.
CORAL: Could you have a look at it for me?
GAYLE: What?
CORAL: Could you read it to me? Tell me what's in it?
> *Pause.*

GAYLE: Can you read, Coral?
CORAL: No. I can't.
> *Pause.*

GAYLE: The reason they want an officer of the Department with you is that there's usually things in there that…
CORAL: I'll be all right.
GAYLE: I know you will. I'm just saying some of the things that are written are not always put in the best way. They're just the way that the caseworker would have written it or so.
CORAL: The reason I wanted one of us. The reason I wanted another Parramatta Girl was because I knew a Parramatta Girl wouldn't squib on me.
GAYLE: Maybe it would be better if one of your friends…
CORAL: Gayle. I'm asking you straight. Read it to me please.
> GAYLE *sits and reads.*

GAYLE: 'Committal to an Institution. Coral Dawn McGillivray. Born 25.9.1947. Charge: Neglect and E.M.D.'

CORAL: Exposed to Moral Danger.
GAYLE: 'Home visit—mother seen. She stated that the girl had not been home for five weeks and that… she did not know where she was.'
CORAL: Read that again.
GAYLE: 'She stated that the girl had not been home for five weeks and that she could not care less what happened to her.'
CORAL: Keep going.
GAYLE: I bet she never said that.
CORAL: Keep going.
GAYLE: 'She stated that she had not reported her missing to the police or the Department because she was not keen to have her found.'
CORAL: She would never have said that.
GAYLE: 'The mother claimed she was not prepared to have her back again, to attend court on her behalf or to take any further interest in her.'
CORAL: And that's a lie.
GAYLE: Of course it is.
CORAL: What else?
GAYLE: 'This is the sworn statement of Monica May Riley, Special Constable of the Women's Police, attached to the Criminal Investigation Brank.'
CORAL: What?
GAYLE: It says brank, but I think it means branch.
CORAL: If it's coppers I think it means brank.

They laugh.

GAYLE: 'At about eight p.m. on the twenty-eighth February this girl was brought to the Women's Police office by Sergeant Sweeney of the Vice Squad. He said, "This is Coral Dawn McGillivray, she is thirteen years old." I said, "Where have you been staying since you left home?" She said, "Residentials, usually Skipton Court of the Durban." I said, "Who has been paying for the room?" She said, "I would go with different men and they would pay." I said, "Have you been having sexual intercourse with these men?" She said, "Yes." I said, "How many?" She said, "I don't know, there were a lot."'

They are both sit silent.

Are you all right?
CORAL: I don't remember any of that.
GAYLE: That's all right.

CORAL: Fancy. [*Pause.*] What does it say about the baby?

GAYLE *looks in the file.*

GAYLE: It just says the date you were discharged. But just because it isn't here doesn't mean anything.

CORAL: They got me to sign something the night I was sent to the 'ospital, she said it was to confirm that I was happy to have the baby at a certain 'ospital, and if I didn't sign she wouldn't be able to take me in the ambulance, and I'd end up having to have my baby at Parramatta without proper maternity facilities. But that paper wasn't about the 'ospital. It was called a 'Socially Cleared' authority. I had signed a paper saying the baby was cleared for adoption. But that's not the end of it. My mother, the one those liars reckon didn't want to take an interest in me, she came with me to the 'ospital. And we got her back. You've got thirty days. You've got thirty days. And so we went to the 'ospital and we screamed blue bloody murder and we got her back.

GAYLE: You went to the hospital?

CORAL: We marched up to that 'ospital and we got her back. I mean, it was more than that.

GAYLE: But you got her back.

CORAL: I got her back. She been with me all these years.

Pause.

GAYLE: You want to know how they discharged me?

CORAL: Yeah.

GAYLE: You sure?

CORAL: Yeah.

GAYLE: Do you remember what the walls of the isolation rooms were?

CORAL: I don't know. They were brick, weren't they?

GAYLE: Raw brick. They left me in there for two days. They didn't check on me for two days. No one will believe that, but they didn't. And when I came out, what I had done was, I had literally, because the walls were raw brick, I had literally stood there and scraped every section, there was not a part of my body I did not scratch on that brick wall. And all they did… I was just covered in mercurochrome the next day. That's all they did was just chuck mercurochrome all over me. [*Beat.*] And you know, on my file, all it says is, 'Gayle fitted into the training situation very smoothly and has maintained a high level of behaviour throughout'.

◆ ◆ ◆ ◆ ◆

SCENE TEN

MARLENE *and* MELANIE *enter.*

MELANIE: Won't never see this place again, I don't reckon.
MARLENE: I know. And I don't know whether to tear it apart with my bare hands or drink it in.
MELANIE: I'm feelin' a lot of anger.
MARLENE: Yep.
MELANIE: Me too.

>MARLENE *is silent.*

I've apologised to my children.
MARLENE: What for?
MELANIE: I was a pretty rough mother.
MARLENE: Rough?

>*Pause.*

MELANIE: I did abuse them.
MARLENE: How?
MELANIE: I hit them.

>MARLENE *is silent.*

Because I didn't know any better.

>MARLENE *is silent.*

But I never left my father alone with my daughter. No way. And when she had her daughter… she didn't know… but I made sure… because he always used to favour my daughter and my daughter's children.

>MARLENE *is silent.*

You too, huh?
MARLENE: What?
MELANIE: You took it out on your children?

>MARLENE *springs over to* MELANIE *and puts her hand over her mouth. She holds it there for long moments. The two women look*

at each other.

MARLENE: Don't you say that.

MELANIE *shakes her head.* MARLENE *takes her hand away.*

Sorry.

MELANIE *holds* MARLENE*'s hand, but roughly by the wrist. She has had enough and it's triggered something off in her.*

MELANIE: Don't you dare try to silence me. Don't you fucking dare try to silence me.

MARLENE: I said I was sorry. I'm sorry. It's just you were saying…

MELANIE: I was saying the truth. The truth. I bashed my kids. You bashed your kids too. I know it. I can see it. You don't have that much anger for that long and not take it out on someone.

MARLENE *is silent.*

We didn't get out of here without scars. We didn't. We didn't survive with our decency intact. We didn't.

Silence.

MARLENE: I'm just so ashamed. I love them so much and I just… used to… Oh, God. I used to scream at them and slap them and belt them with a leather strap. I had this leather strap with beads that came from Fiji and I used to belt them so hard that all the beads broke and went flying all over the place.

MELANIE: But you regret what you did.

MARLENE: Oh, I regret it so much. I regret it so much. And I look at this place. And I smell this disinfectant and this place.

MELANIE: You can apologise to your kids.

MARLENE: No.

MELANIE: Yes. You can.

MARLENE: And who's going to say sorry to me? Who's going to say sorry for all the things that were done to me and can't be undone?

Pause.

MELANIE: I'm sorry.

A long pause.

MARLENE: Thank you.

Pause.

MELANIE: The old hankie's been gettin' a work out today, hasn't it?

Genevieve Hegney as Maree in the 2007 Company B production in Sydney. (Photo: Heidrun Löhr)

MARLENE: Sure has.

> MELANIE *reaches out and shakes* MARLENE's *hand, a strengthening.*

MELANIE: Come on, I hear there's gonna be sandwiches.
MARLENE: I wasn't told to bring a plate.
MELANIE: No, DOCS are providing it.
MARLENE: [*with a laugh*] Good old Coral, eh. Got the Department to spring for sandwiches.

◆ ◆ ◆ ◆ ◆

SCENE ELEVEN

MAREE *and* LYNETTE *enter.*

LYNETTE: I didn't recognise you.
MAREE: Like Mary.
LYNETTE: Who?
MAREE: Mary. At the tomb. She didn't recognise Christ. At first. When he was resurrected. Not until he touched her and said her name, 'Mary'.
LYNETTE: Maree. [*Beat.*] I'm glad you came back.
MAREE: I didn't get to say goodbye.
LYNETTE: I wasn't worth it.
MAREE: I wasn't.
LYNETTE: I let you down.

> MAREE *is silent.*

I didn't know the first thing about the kind of life you'd had.

> LYNETTE *touches her own face.*

MAREE: Don't touch me.
LYNETTE: Will that make you disappear?
MAREE: No, I don't want you to get any of my bad luck on you.
LYNETTE: It's not catching.
MAREE: Oh, I think it is.

> *Pause.*

LYNETTE: I loved you, Maree. I loved you and I miss you.

MAREE: You shouldn't say that.
LYNETTE: I loved you.
MAREE: I was just a waste of space.
LYNETTE: Not to me.
MAREE: All of us were. Rubbish.
LYNETTE: I would have loved you.
MAREE: What a waste that would have been.

>MAREE *exits.*
>
>CORAL, MARLENE *and* JUDI *enter with a trolley of tea and sandwiches.* KERRY *enters from the other side of the stage. She calls* MARLENE *over.*

KERRY: Marlene.
MARLENE: Kerry. You right?
KERRY: Just a bit nervous. About the speech.
MARLENE: I didn't know you were giving a speech.
KERRY: No. No one else does neither.
MARLENE: What d'ya mean?
KERRY: They're gonna have the speeches in a moment.
MARLENE: And?
KERRY: And I wanna talk about how it got closed down.
MARLENE: So. Who's gonna stop ya?
KERRY: The Department.
MARLENE: What?
KERRY: The Reunion Committee.
MARLENE: Why would they?
KERRY: I asked them can I tell about the closing down and they said, 'If we let you speak everyone will want to, and you do go on, Kerry.' [*Pause.*] Well, do I?
MARLENE: What?
KERRY: Go on?

>Pause.

MARLENE: Just grab the microphone.
KERRY: Really?
MARLENE: I better see you making that speech, sister.

◆ ◆ ◆ ◆ ◆

SCENE TWELVE

GAYLE *takes her seat. She looks at* JUDI *but then moves away.* JUDI *goes over to* LYNETTE.

JUDI: [*indicating* GAYLE] There she is.
LYNETTE: Who?
JUDI: The one who recognised me.
LYNETTE: So go speak to her.
JUDI: No.
LYNETTE: There's only today. You have to do it now. You'll never, never get the chance to see these women again.
JUDI: So. I can live with it.
LYNETTE: You've been living with it. All these years. Put it down. Put it down today in this place.

> JUDI *is silent.*

There'll be good intentions. There'll be talk of staying in touch. But you won't. This is it.

> JUDI *shakes her head.*

Then I dare you.
JUDI: What?
LYNETTE: You're a Parramatta Girl. You know what a dare means.
JUDI: I'm not going to respond to that. I'm not sixteen.
LYNETTE: Then you won't mind if I call you a gutless little whore.

> *There is a long silence where they look at each other.* JUDI *goes over to* GAYLE.

JUDI: I am the one who… did what you said I did.
GAYLE: I know.

> *Pause.*

JUDI: I changed my name to Judi. My name when I was in here was Fay McKell.
GAYLE: Never forget a face.
JUDI: Right.
GAYLE: Come to offer me your confession, did you?
JUDI: No.
GAYLE: 'Course you did.

> *Pause.*

JUDI: Well, what would be so wrong if I did want to talk about it?
GAYLE: Wouldn't be wrong. Just be typical.
> *Pause.*

JUDI: This is not possible.
GAYLE: Well, thank you, Your Highness, the arbiter of what's possible.
JUDI: How can you be so hard?
GAYLE: Me? I'm harder than the inside of a nun's mattress.
> *Pause.*

LYNETTE: Come on, Judi.
JUDI: What?
LYNETTE: Maybe I was wrong to suggest it.
GAYLE: So you needed prompting, then? To own up?
JUDI: I just wanted to speak to you.
> *Pause.* JUDI *begins to leave.*

GAYLE: When you played the role of Portia, that's when we knew.
JUDI: You remember that?
GAYLE: I remember you never came to any of the auditions, or the read-through, and then there you were, large as life, with the lead role. You knew your way around a wrinkly, old dick before the rest of us knew our way around a box of tampons.
JUDI: Wheras you wouldn't say dick if your mouth was full of it.
GAYLE: You thought you were so good in them bloody plays.
JUDI: I was good.
GAYLE: You were shit. Wooden shit.
JUDI: I was not. The ABC taped us.
GAYLE: The ABC thought you were shit.
JUDI: They did not.
LYNETTE: Come on, Judi.
> *Pause.*

JUDI: What else do you remember?
LYNETTE: Judi.
JUDI: Nothin'. She remembers stuff, that's all.
> LYNETTE *raises her eyebrows.*

Yeah, well maybe we'll never be best friends.
GAYLE: You can take that as gospel.
LYNETTE: Fine.

JUDI *nods.* LYNETTE *exits. Pause.*

JUDI: Do you remember the Hungarian matron?
GAYLE: My good girl jest.
JUDI: My good girl jest. What the hell did that mean?
GAYLE: It meant you were in trouble.
JUDI: To this day I don't know what it means.

They fall into a silence.

GAYLE: Two squares of toilet paper for a piss and six for a shit.
JUDI: What was your number?
GAYLE: Nine-seven-six. You?
JUDI: One-one-five.

Pause.

GAYLE: Louise Ferino. Came in at the same time as little Ilona Verona.
JUDI: Ilona Verona. I remember her. She was the little Italian girl who poisoned her parents.
GAYLE: Louise Ferino took me under her wing. She told me, you've gotta have a bit of guts, you've gotta fight back, because I'd just stand there and take it. Anyway… I started to. One night in the toilets… two girls got me in the toilets and I fought back and I beat them. And that's when I started to get a little bit of power myself. I had that experience of 'It's me against the world'. [*Pause.*] Go on, then.
JUDI: What?
GAYLE: Say it.
JUDI: Say what?
GAYLE: Say, 'And ya still do'.

JUDI *takes her card out of her bag and hands it to* GAYLE.

Changed your name. Why'd you do that?
JUDI: Too many people knew me from working.
GAYLE: Tarot reader, clairvoyant, astrologer, numerologist, rebirther, counsellor. Professional psychic since 1973. Psychic, eh? Did ya know I was gonna be here, then?
JUDI: Not really.
GAYLE: Eh? Come on.
JUDI: Or someone like you.
GAYLE: True?
JUDI: You or someone like you. I hoped.
GAYLE: 'It is better to light candles than to curse the darkness.'

JUDI: Don't you think?

They stand, awkward, not knowing how to take their leave of each other. JUDI *puts her hand out.* GAYLE *looks at it, long and hard.* JUDI *drops her hand. But* GAYLE *doesn't leave. They stand there, awkward.*

JUDI: Did you find the dungeons?
GAYLE: Yep.
JUDI: Is that what you called the showers?
GAYLE: No. Other side from the showers. Vacant rooms from when it was an orphanage. If you were never taken there you would have never known. [*Beat.*] So why'd you do it, why'd you go with the Super?
JUDI: I was out for myself. And I knew it was coming. So I brought it on myself.
GAYLE: That's how they get you. There's this little doubt, this little fear that you did something to bring it on yourself.
JUDI: Well, in my case, I did.
GAYLE: Yeah, but who was the adult, Judi?

JUDI *is silent.*

Who was the adult?
JUDI: No, I can't blame him.
GAYLE: Who was the adult?
JUDI: I knew what I was doing.
GAYLE: At sixteen?
JUDI: Yeah. But I've forgiven myself.
GAYLE: Who was the adult?
JUDI: It's not that simple.
GAYLE: It's always that simple. They want to make it all grey and complicated. But, really, it wasn't different in those days. It wasn't that times have changed. It doesn't matter if it was ten years ago or fifty years ago or a thousand years ago. It has never been right to sexually abuse a child. Never. Don't let them tell you it's complicated.
JUDI: It was wrong?
GAYLE: It was wrong.

JUDI *sits for a long moment to consider, understand, and accept what* GAYLE *has said. Finally, she seems to come back into herself. She leans forward and embraces* GAYLE.

♦ ♦ ♦ ♦ ♦

SCENE THIRTEEN

All the other girls come on stage.

CORAL: Listen to me. [*She stands on steps or something that raises her up.*] Can all of you listen to me? Especially you Parramatta Girls. I know you're women, but you'll always be girls to me. My name is Coral and I was here in the sixties. About ten generations of girls was locked up in 'ere. And after they spat us out we became the mothers and sisters and wives of Australia. Sometimes there was an 'undred of us in here, sometimes there was two 'undred. Well, my maths has never been very good and you know why that is. But maths or no maths, two hundred girls by eighty years is a lot to answer for. We've got something in common, ladies. Something in common and we're gonna share it today. Some of you have come from Queensland, England, all over, to be here. Some of you are here alone, some of you have brought your families. On behalf of the Reunion Committee I want to welcome you.

The girls clap. MARLENE *wheels a copper onto the stage. All the girls ooh and ah.*

When I was in here, we washed everything in a copper. So what we're gonna do is this. Lynette here, is gonna give you a small sheet, we got them from the Department, and you're gonna tear them up, into small pieces. You'll enjoy that. When you've got your bit of sheet, I'm gonna come round and give you a texta and you're gonna write on it something you wanna let go of. Maybe a memory. Maybe a person you want to honour, but put to rest. Maybe you want to give thanks for one of the staff who was kind to you. You decide. It's your bit of sheet. Then you're gonna put that in this copper, stir it around a little, and then ring it out through here. And then you can hang it up here, on this clothesline we've put up. So after we leave today, the black of the texta will still be on the copper and the dirty laundry will be washed clean. Simple as that. If you don't like it, don't do it. But if you wanna do it, get over here and get yourself a piece of sheet.

All the women, in turn, take a sheet. They have fun tearing them into small strips.

CORAL *hands them textas and they silently write on the pieces of*

> sheet all the things they want to let go of. KERRY *jumps up and takes the microphone.*

KERRY: I was in here. I was part of getting this GTS closed down. That came about... I found out later through the interview. The girl's name was Shirley Donlan. She was in the isolation cell next to me. She came from a pretty well-to-do family. Now when she went home, she was complaining of a sore jaw to her mother. Her mother took her to a doctor's. The doctor said she had gangrene in her jaw. And her mother's gone, well she's just come from Parramatta Girls Home two days ago, could that have happened in the last two days? And the doctor's gone, no, this must have been going on for months. So that musta started an investigation, like. And when I was called in to the office to do the interview, I went in and the room was just full of cops, you know. Okay, 'Kerry, do you remember being in an isolation cell?' And they gave me a date. And I said, 'Look, I've been in isolation a lot of times.' 'Well, tell us about the day you were beside Shirley Donlan. What happened?' Well, I remember hearing the door open, Shirley and I let one another know that they were coming in. We didn't know whose cell he was going into. He went into Shirley's. She sung out to me, 'My turn.' And next minute I started hearing thud, thud, and about five minutes of it before I could hear her crying and screaming to stop, that's enough. And I remember hearing him asking an officer, 'Don't forget to tell me if someone's coming.' And then I was asked, 'Have any of the male officers ever hit you more than a father would hit his child for doing something wrong?' And I've gone, 'What do you mean? How hard does a daddy hit his little girl? I don't know. I've got no mum and dad, I've only ever known this life. This system. I'm a Ward of the State. How hard does a daddy hit his little girl?'

> MARLENE *makes an encouraging thumbs-up motion to* KERRY *to keep her going.*

So then they said, 'Okay, thanks Kerry, you just sign this. I signed something. God knows what I signed, and I was told to go to my dormitory. I was not to repeat any of the things I said to any of the other girls. Two weeks later I was sittin' on Parramatta Road with twenty-one dollars, which was what was equivalent to the dole then, the address of two girls hostels and two foster families that were willing to um… let me board. And goodbye. Two weeks after I signed those statements. Why? About six months after that, the home closed down altogether.

The women all clap. KERRY *looks chuffed.*

LYNETTE: I wanna say something too. I want us to take a moment, ladies, for our friend Maree Seddon who hung herself off the end of a doorknob in Dormitory Two. This one's for all the women who didn't make it through because of this place, and those who didn't make it to today because of the scars that Parramatta left on them.

As the women each complete their task of 'washing out a memory' LYNETTE *sings 'The Singing Bird', then it is taken up by* MAREE *singing, just visible on the opposite side of the stage.*

[*Singing*] I have seen the lark soar high at morn,
Heard his song up in the blue,
I have heard the blackbird pipe his note,
The thrush and the linnet too.

But there's none of them can sing so sweet,
My singing bird as you.
If I could lure my singing bird
From his own cosy nest.

If I could catch my singing bird,
I would warm him on my breast.
For there's none of them can sing so sweet
My singing bird as you.

They finish singing.

JUDI *goes to a door on the set and tries to open it to go out. The door is locked. She looks around and gives a little laugh, then tries the door again. She becomes agitated and tries to open it using more force. Then she begins to bang on it and wrench it back and forth.*

JUDI: Hello? Hello? Someone? Is someone there? I need to get out of here now. Hello? Hello? Will someone please let me out of here? Please? I'm not supposed to be in here. Let me out. Let me out. Please let me out.

She bashes on the door and then stops and checks her elbows.

She hurriedly begins to unwrap the bandages, unravelling them desperately from both arms. She gets bound up in the bandages and begins crying and rocking, jolted out of her self by the panic attack she is experiencing. CORAL *comes over to her.*

CORAL: Come on, Judi love.

JUDI: I can't get out, they've locked us in.

CORAL *goes to the door and opens it.*

CORAL: Look.

JUDI *goes over and sees that she can get out.*

JUDI: Silly old girl.

CORAL: Look, you can go out anytime you want.

JUDI: And then my elbows.

CORAL: Your what?

She checks her elbows but there's nothing wrong with them. CORAL *rolls up her sleeves and shows* JUDI *her healed elbows. Behind them all the women roll up their sleeves and check their elbows and wave them in the air.* JUDI *laughs.* GAYLE *steps forward.*

GAYLE: I've done a lot of good with my life. I had a hotel at Lakemba—we managed a hotel for a very, very famous boxer, Vic Patrick. He was the world lightweight champion a long, long time ago. Lovely, lovely man. Anyrate, I was walking with my Amanda, in the stroller, Belinda wasn't born then, and I was approached by a scout from the Lovely Motherhood Quest. Can you believe it? Well, get this for a joke, I did it. I entered the competition—I had… because by then we were so well into the surf club—so we could have lots of functions to raise money for the deaf and blind kiddies. And do you know what? Do you know what? I bloody won it. I won it and to this day I think that's my greatest achievement… Not for the Motherhood Award but for being the Charity Queen and raising the most money. And that was the thing that I really felt proud of myself. I worked like a dog, you know. But I did it, Loveliest Mother. How about that? [*Pause.*] Loveliest Mother. And me a Parramatta Girl.

The lights fade.

THE END

Eyes to the Floor
Remembering the Hay Girls Home

Alana Valentine

Kayla Barrett as Marjorie in the 2008 Outback Theatre production. (Photo: James Edwards)

Writer's Note

It was when I began researching the stories of women who were incarcerated in the Girls Training School, Parramatta, formerly known as the Parramatta Girls Home, that I first began to hear stories of Hay. Women in their fifties, sixties, seventies and even eighties would sit across from me, having revealed the most gruesome and horrifying recollections of their time at Parramatta, and then they would say the word. Hay. After what I had heard it did not seem possible that there could be a place of which they had been more afraid, of which they spoke of in even more hushed and fearful tones. Some who had been there, others who had been threatened with the place and seen the effect on other inmates who returned to Parramatta. And where the stories about Parramatta had flowed out of them—jagged, brutal, struggling into the light often after many, many years of silence—the stories about Hay were harder to speak aloud. Often it was just a look of utter pain and despair, a quiet shaking of the head as if the horror of the recollection was just too incomprehensible, too appalling to form into syllables. But then these astonishingly courageous women, these women whom I have come to respect with such deep and abiding awe, these strong and beautiful survivors, gave voice to their memories and trusted me with their feelings and their stories. And a picture began to emerge of an injustice so grotesque that I could only sit open-mouthed and weeping that such treatment had been metered out to Australian children until as recently as 1974.

As with my stage play *Parramatta Girls*, the characters here are composites from all the stories I have been told by actual survivors of these two institutions, as well as from material on the public record in newspapers, the Senate report 'Forgotten Australians' and from interviews with counsellors and psychologists who treat the legacy of such incarcerations. All of the characters are fictional and do not represent any particular individual, but all of the stories are true and were drawn from one or another of the above sources. I would especially like to thank the former employees of the Hay Girls Institution who told me their own stories with candour and sincerity. I wanted to include their perspective because of the central thesis of this play, which is that a brutal state institution like this leaves a painful legacy, most especially on the former inmates themselves, but also on their families, the guards who were employed to work there, the town of Hay, and, in ways too numerous to calibrate, on the complexion of Australia's past and its future. I have profound admiration for the town of Hay for confronting and supporting this examination of old wounds and painful histories. I commemorate the women who died carrying the burden of a childhood broken by violence and abuse in institutions such as Hay. I dedicate this play to those working with Australian children today, under what must always be enormously difficult circumstances, to provide some better way forward for neglected and troubled young women and girls.

Alana Valentine
April 2008

Eyes to the Floor first previewed at the Hay Goal Museum on 26 April 2008 and was first produced by Outback Theatre for Young People in association with Griffith Regional Theatre at the Griffith Regional Theatre, Griffith on 2 May 2008, with the following cast:

MARJORIE	Kayla Barrett
FIONA	Danielle Curtis
GWEN	Ebony Lees
EMMA	Teleaha Marlin
JANE	Abby Martin
DANIELLA	Alannah Robertson
FUREDI/LENNY/HAWKINS	Jack Murray
GUARD KAY	Ashleigh Haynes-Holyoake
MR NAYLOR	Craig Higgs

Director, Amy Hardingham
Choreographer, Lee Pemberton
Set/Costume Designer, Nicola Barber
Sound Designer, Scott Howie
Lighting Designer, John Matkovic
Production/Stage Manager, Sophie Berry
OTYP Company Manager, Carlie Mason
Photography/Video, James Edwards
Costume Realisation, Elizabeth Howe, Kayla Barrett, Linda Wright

CHARACTERS

DANIELLA GREAVES 15, Hay inmate

JANE ROGERS 16, Hay inmate

EMMA ABBOT 14, Hay inmate

GWEN GILL 16, Hay inmate

FIONA HODGES 17, Hay inmate

MARJORIE LINNETT 17, Hay inmate

GUARD FUREDI, guard at Hay

FH HAWKINS, Minister for Child and Social Welfare

LENNY

MRS KAY, A recently arrived guard at Hay

MR NAYLOR, Superintendent at Hay

FATHER

The actor who plays FUREDI also plays HAWKINS and LENNY.
The actor who plays NAYLOR also plays FATHER.
The play is set in the remembered past.

SCENE ONE

FIONA *stands alone on stage. She holds a long lead with a single light bulb on it. She holds the bulb up to her face and then swings the bulb back and forth across her face. Finally she spins the globe in circles around her head.*

FIONA: Committal to an Institution. Fiona June Hodges. Born 22.2.1944. Charge: Neglected and Exposed to Moral Danger.

> JANE *enters the stage. She too has a long lead with a single bulb and performs the same actions as* FIONA.

JANE: Committal to an Institution: Jane Dawn Rogers. Born 19.6.1945. Charge: Neglect and Exposed to Moral Danger.

> EMMA *enters the stage. She too has a long lead with a single bulb and performs the same actions as* JANE.

EMMA: Committal to an Institution: Emma Abbot. Born 21.8.1947. Charge: Uncontrollable. Escape from Cootamundra Girls Home.

> GWEN *enters the stage. She too has a long lead with a single bulb and performs the same actions as* EMMA.

GWEN: Committal to an Institution: Gwen Gill. Born 9.3.1945. Charge: Uncontrollable. Escape from Cootamundra Girls Home.

> MARJORIE *enters the stage. She too has a long lead with a single bulb and performs the same actions as* GWEN.

MARJORIE: Committal to an Institution: Marjorie Linnett. Born 6.11.1944. Charge: Uncontrollable and Exposed to Moral Danger.

> DANIELLA *enters the stage. She too has a long lead with a single bulb and performs the same actions as* MARJORIE.

DANIELLA: Committal to an Institution: Daniella Andrea Greaves. Born 14.5.1946. Charge: Uncontrollable and exposed to Moral Danger.

FIONA: General Comment: Last Saturday afternoon it became apparent that Hodges had assumed leadership of the girls and the recreation period was very disturbed by her. Girls who previously were conforming satisfactorily became troublesome.

JANE: Home situation: The home is a fibro-lined tin shack in a poor state of repair. Home contains two tiny rooms. One is a kitchen where the father sleeps, in the other room, Jane, Louise and baby shared one bed, three younger boys share second bed and two eldest boys share third bed.

EMMA: Home situation: Emma had been removed from home when father charged with shooting uncle in the thigh.

GWEN: Home situation: Became a ward of the state at six months old. Was living with a foster family, the Anthonys who commented that her behaviour whilst in the home could not be faulted, but her behaviour outside was most undesirable and they had not been able to control her.

MARJORIE: Home Situation: Father still caring for large family of brothers and sisters after mother died of cancer one year ago. Father seems to have taken to drinking after this event, eventually being jailed for fighting.

DANIELLA: Home Situation: Daniella lives in desperate poverty in Surry Hills, Sydney.

FIONA: Although the crisis has passed the influence of Hodges is such that it will be several weeks before the effect of her time in the main institution is erased.

JANE: There is a bare minimum of furniture. Mrs Rogers has applied for a Housing commission home and lives in hopes of getting it.

EMMA: Emma was being housed at Cootamundra Girls home then, with two other girls jumped a goods train and was carried as far as Narrandera before being apprehended by the local police constable.

GWEN: Gwen was being housed at Cootamundra Girls home then, with two other girls jumped a goods train and was carried as far as Narrandera before being apprehended by the local police constable.

MARJORIE: Three youngest sisters placed in an orphanage by sister-in-law and Marjorie was employed in a factory at thirteen when subsequently charged with neglect and exposed to moral danger by sister-in-law.

DANIELLA: She has been treated for repeated sexual assaults at a young age, one of which resulted in a pregnancy and the birth of a child who has been adopted out.

FIONA: Recommendation:

All begin their lines in unison.

FIONA: That Fiona June Hodges be transferred from the Training

School Parramatta to the Institution for Girls, Hay. Transfer Order herewith for Minister's signature.

JANE: Jane has been repeatedly reprimanded for language infringements at Parramatta and transferred to Hay on 26.10.61. Transfer order herewith for Minister's signature.

EMMA: Transferred to Parramatta and thence to Hay for repeated charge of refusing duties. Transfer order herewith for Minister's signature.

GWEN: Transferred to Parramatta and thence to Hay for repeated charge of refusing duties. Transfer order herewith for Minister's signature.

MARJORIE: Committed to Parramatta by Sydney Children's Court and transferred to 'The Institution for Girls, Hay' for repeated self-mutilation. Transfer order herewith for Minister's signature.

DANIELLA: Committed to Parramatta by Sydney Children's Court and transferred to Hay after repeated twenty-four hour detentions for violent, uncontrollable behaviour at Parramatta. Transfer order herewith for Minister's signature.

All the GIRLS *being to say 'Choo Choo, Bum Bum' in unison, as a chanting rhythm. It becomes quicker and more insistent until it cross fades with the sound of a train.*

The GIRLS *run past* FIONA *with their lights, as if lights passing outside the window and the chanting continues. The other* GIRLS *force* FIONA *to drink largactyl. She staggers around, disorientated.*

FIONA: I am scared to death
And wish that I could sleep.
The rocking of the train lulls me
Dulls me.
Between stations there is time
Expressed in forward motion
And there is
Gentle
Fragmental
Sleep
My limbs are heavy with it
My eyes droop
How delicious is the oblivion of dreams
Those palaces of imagination

How I long to slip into the silk of rest
Of sleep
Of glorious rest
But now I feel the train lurch
A sign flashes by
Narrandera
And I am being
bundled into a truck
It is close, it is airless
Again we lurch
And I feel the speed increase
I cannot rest
I cannot sleep
The speed increases
They do as they please
They do as they like
And still the pace
Escalates
Even more
Even more
I am lost.

> FIONA *finally falls to the ground and all the other characters leave the stage.*

❖ ❖ ❖ ❖ ❖

SCENE TWO

SUPERINTENDENT NAYLOR, *in a suit and tie, stands beside the fallen* FIONA. *He kicks her, casually, and she groggily wakes up. She looks up at him.*

NAYLOR: Rule Number One. Don't look at me. Don't ever look at me. I repeat. Don't ever look me in the eye.

> FIONA *gets up onto her feet, she is unsteady but looks at the ground.*

NAYLOR: Do you understand?
FIONA: Yes.

NAYLOR: Right. That is called a bounce.
FIONA: A what?
NAYLOR: A bounce. You'll have no sweets with your dinner this evening.
FIONA: For what?
NAYLOR: For looking me in the eye.
FIONA: [*looking up*] I didn't.

>NAYLOR *meets her eye.*

NAYLOR: That's half your dinner this evening gone.

>FIONA *looks at the ground.*

Am I making myself understood?
FIONA: Yes.
NAYLOR: Yes, who?
FIONA: Yes, Superintendent.
NAYLOR: There was a girl brought in yesterday, name of Jane Rogers.
FIONA: Sir.
NAYLOR: She lost both her dinner and her sweets last evening.

>*Pause.* FIONA *continues to look at the ground.*

She was given bread and water and put in isolation for twenty-four hours.

>FIONA *looks up.* NAYLOR *meets her gaze.*

Once more and you will be put in isolation yourself.

>*The tough nut almost cracks. Her chin wobbles but she doesn't cry.*

FIONA: I'm sorry, sir.
NAYLOR: Yes, I'm sorry too.

>FIONA *stands, eyes still to the ground.*

♦ ♦ ♦ ♦ ♦

SCENE THREE

GUARD FUREDI *blows a whistle.*

FUREDI: All rise.

>*The* GIRLS *rise from their beds. Their clothing is passed to them through a flap which is then relocked. In perfect unison, the*

> GIRLS *get out of bed, take off their nightdresses, fold them, tie them with tape and place them with their reading matter on the bed. They get dressed and then stand at the head of the bed.*
>
> *All the cell doors are opened and* FUREDI *inspects the beds for tidiness. The* GIRLS, *without exception, have their eyes to the floor.*

Kneel.

> *The* GIRLS, *simultaneously, kneel.*

GIRLS: Our Father,
Who Art in Heaven,
Hallowed be thy name,
Thy kingdom come,
Thy will be done on earth
As it is in heaven.
Give us this day our daily bread
And forgive us our trespasses,
As we forgive those who trespass against us
Lead us not into temptation
But deliver us from evil
For thine is the kingdom, the power and the glory,
For ever and ever,
Amen.

FUREDI: Stand.

> *The* GIRLS, *in unison, stand at attention, facing the bed.*

Gear up.

> *The* GIRLS *pick up their nightwear, night can and reading material.*

Move.

> *The* GIRLS *move to the cabin doorways.*

Daniella Greaves.

DANIELLA: Yes, Mr Furedi.

> DANIELLA *goes to her locker, place her night attire on the shelf and picks up her comb and toothbrush. She then moves back to the cell door.*

Reporting back to you Mr Furedi.

FUREDI: Marjorie Linnett.

MARJORIE: Yes, Mr Furedi.

> MARJORIE *goes to her locker, places her night attire on the shelf and picks up her comb and toothbrush. She then moves back to the cell door.*

FUREDI: Fiona Hodges.
FIONA: [*quietly*] Yes, Mr Furedi.
FUREDI: What?
FIONA: Well, you know who I am, don't you?
FUREDI: That's twenty minutes of practices, Hodges. [*Pause.*] What did you say?
FIONA: Yes, Mr Furedi.

> FIONA *goes to her locker, places her night attire on the shelf, picks up her comb and toothbrush. She then moves back to the cell door.*

FUREDI: Jane Rogers.
JANE: Yes, Mr Furedi.

> JANE *goes to her locker, places her night attire on the shelf, picks up her comb and toothbrush. She then moves back to the cell door.*

FUREDI: Daniella Greaves.
DANIELLA: Yes, Mr Furedi.

> DANIELLA *moves to another part of the stage to shower. Before she does so she reports to the* GUARD *there.*

Reporting to you, Mrs Kay.
MRS KAY: Carry on.

> DANIELLA *then empties her night can, uses the toilet, washes and cleans her teeth. When she is finished she returns to* MRS KAY.

DANIELLA: Reporting to you, Mrs Kay.
MRS KAY: Carry on.

> DANIELLA *then collects her cabin cleaning gear, moves to her locker, replaces the comb and toothbrush and then goes back to her cell door.*

DANIELLA: Reporting back to you, Mr Furedi.

> *As all the* GIRLS *go through this routine they will finish one*

by one and end by standing at their cell doors. Once all are assembled NAYLOR, who has entered to observe, directs them.

NAYLOR: Move.

The GIRLS *all, simultaneously, take three steps into their cells. The doors are then closed and locked by the officers, but the flap on the cell is left open.*

The two OFFICERS *come and serve breakfast through the flap.*

SCENE FOUR

EMMA *and* GWEN *are together.*

EMMA: They normally transport you separately.
GWEN: Yeah, so.
EMMA: So, there must be a reason they put us together.
GWEN: Not that reason.
EMMA: How do you know?
GWEN: Because. [*Beat.*] Why would they know that?
EMMA: It'd be in their files. From when you was taken away.
GWEN: Nah.
EMMA: Yeah, they got it all written down. On bits of paper in them files. They've got our whole lives in them files.
GWEN: Then why don't they tell us?
EMMA: Because. They don't want us to know. But I'm smarter than them. I've worked it out.

Pause.

GWEN: So would they have written down all the stuff about Cootamundra?
EMMA: Yeah. For sure.
GWEN: How we met up there and then tried to escape?
EMMA: Yeah.
GWEN: How you fell off the train and sprained your ankle?
EMMA: That rattler was too high for me.
GWEN: So I shouldn't have brung ya.
EMMA: Well why did ya?
GWEN: You said you wanted to come.

EMMA: I did. Because of who you are.
> *Pause.*

GWEN: How do you know?
EMMA: 'Cause ya look like me.
GWEN: That's no proof.
EMMA: You got the same eyes.
GWEN: That's no proof.
EMMA: I just know.
GWEN: Ya can't just know.
EMMA: I do. That's why I helped ya in Parramatta.
GWEN: You shouldn'ta done that.
EMMA: You gotta take care of me. We gotta take care of each other.
GWEN: Yeah.
EMMA: You do.
GWEN: Says who?
EMMA: Says me.
GWEN: So. Why should I listen to you?
> *Pause.*

EMMA: Because I'm your sister.
GWEN: Are not.
EMMA: I am.
> *Pause.*

GWEN: So. Even if you are. And that's only a maybe.
EMMA: So.
GWEN: So. So what?
EMMA: So, sisters look after each other and nothing can separate them.
GWEN: Yeah it can.
> GWEN *grabs* EMMA *and hauls her up by the collar.*

Don't you ever say anything to anyone about your theory.
EMMA: I won't.
GWEN: Anyone who gets me into trouble, I'll pay them back.

♦ ♦ ♦ ♦ ♦

SCENE FIVE

NAYLOR *and* FUREDI *are onstage when* MRS KAY *enters, holding a broken piece of the concrete path.*

MRS KAY: I wouldn't have believed it.
NAYLOR: What's that?
MRS KAY: But now I've seen it for myself.
NAYLOR: Sorry?
MRS KAY: I've seen what these little terrors can do.
NAYLOR: Is that part of the path?
MRS KAY: So how did they get away from you?
NAYLOR: To do what?
MRS KAY: To break up the path. I mean, was there a riot? What did they use?
NAYLOR: Pick axes.
MRS KAY: But where were they hiding them? I watch them at night. I watch them. I've never seen pick axes.
NAYLOR: We gave them the pick axes.

Pause.

MRS KAY: What?
NAYLOR: We gave them the pick axes to break up the path.
MRS KAY: But they've just laid the path.
NAYLOR: And now they can lay it again. [*He take the lump of concrete from* MRS KAY *and throws it in the air and catches it a few times.*] Mrs Kay. [*Beat.*] It's a discipline exercise.

Pause.

MRS KAY: It's a stupid exercise.
NAYLOR: As you said yourself ... they're terrors.
MRS KAY: Many of them can't read or write.
NAYLOR: Exactly.
MRS KAY: So let me teach them.
NAYLOR: We all think that, at first.
MRS KAY: Think what? That they could benefit from learning to read?
NAYLOR: But then you see what they are.
MRS KAY: Uneducated, disadvantaged, neglected children.
NAYLOR: Morally misguided, sexual extroverts, violent, unstable terrors.

MRS KAY: Then give them rehabilitation.

NAYLOR: They don't deserve to be given anything else. Parramatta tried to give them guidance and what did they do? These girls climbed on the roof and hurled roof tiles at their protectors. These girls swallowed pins and needles and brasso to get away from the people who were trying to help them. These girls, these ten girls are the worst, most violent, unstable girls in New South Wales and you want to mollycoddle them?

MRS KAY: I was only suggesting some arithmetic.

NAYLOR: They are taught to wash floors, they are taught to wash clothes, they are taught to assist in the kitchen. When you see them they're locked behind bars, sleeping but we live with the fact that they can turn any moment into little wildcats who could scratch your eyes out if you let them get close to you.

MRS KAY: You don't think they're going to do that.

NAYLOR: I do think they're going to do that if we give them the chance. If we underestimate them. The system has tried to help them. We didn't ask their parents to abandon them, we didn't ask them to run away from home, we didn't ask them to give themselves to their boyfriends or assist in armed robberies or destroy and burn government property at Parramatta. Why do they deserve to be treated well?

MRS KAY: It might reform them.

NAYLOR: I don't believe that. I don't believe that they are capable of change. They are vicious little bitches who won't do as they're told. Take off your rose-coloured glasses.

> *He throws the lump of rock in the air again but this time he misses catching it and it smashes on the ground.* MRS KAY *begins to exit but stops as* NAYLOR *speaks.*

Religious instruction. Not religious discussion. Not religious conversion. You may instruct them, Mrs Kay. [*Beat.*] That is what you may do for us and for the community who will be forced to live with them.

> MRS KAY *leaves, then* NAYLOR *exits, passing an entering* FIONA *as she goes.*

FUREDI: Commence practice.

> FIONA *stands.*

Eyes to the floor.

FIONA *marches back and forth across the stage, back and forth back and forth.*

Cease practice.

FIONA *stands at attention.*

Commence practice.

FIONA: Yes, Mr Furedi.
Yes, Mr Furedi.
Yes, Mr Furedi.

FUREDI: Cease practice.
Yes, Mr Furedi. Like you mean it.
Commence practice.

FIONA: Yes, Mr Furedi.
Yes, Mr Furedi.
Yes, Mr Furedi.
Yes, Mr Furedi.

FUREDI: Cease practice.

FIONA *stands at attention.*

Commence practice.

FIONA *picks up a pile of clothes and folds them. She shakes them out and folds them again. She shakes them out and folds them again. She shakes them out and folds them again.*

Cease practice.

FUREDI *goes over and folds the cloth, very carefully.*

Commence practice.

FIONA *folds the clothes again. Over and over.*

Cease practice.

FIONA *stands at attention.*

FIONA: Reporting to you, Mr Furedi

FUREDI *is holding an orange. He drops it and stands on it.*

FUREDI: Permission to eat your fruit.

FIONA *picks up and eats the fruit.*

♦ ♦ ♦ ♦ ♦

SCENE SIX

The GIRLS *move into the dining room in single file, at intervals of two metres apart. They proceed to their nominated place at the table and mark time.*

FUREDI: Halt.

> *The* GIRLS *stop marking time.*

Sit.

> *The* GIRLS *sit. Two girls,* JANE *and* MARJORIE, *carry meals from the servery and place them in front of the* GIRLS *who are seated.*

Grace.

DANIELLA: For what we are about to receive may the Lord make us truly thankful.

> DANIELLA *sits down. The* GIRLS *sit, waiting.* NAYLOR *enters with* MRS KAY. *The* GIRLS *do not look up at her.*

NAYLOR: Carry on.

> *The meal proceeds in silence. As each* GIRL *finishes she puts her knife and fork on the top of the plate.*

FUREDI: Grace.

> DANIELLA *stands.*

DANIELLA: Thank you for the world so sweet
Thank you for the food we eat.
Thank you for the birds that sing.
Thank you God for everything.

> DANIELLA *sits down.*

> JANE *and* MARJORIE, *now clear the plates and put them in a servery. The* GIRLS *stand and line up, as in muster.*

NAYLOR: First, I remind you that girls are to sleep facing the door at all times. I have been receiving reports that too many girls, too often are rolling over in their sleep. These girls will be woken, made to stand for an hour until they learn to sleep facing the door. Do you understand?

GIRLS: Yes, Superintendent.

NAYLOR: What?

GIRLS: [*more loudly*] Yes, Superintendent.

NAYLOR: Second. You have a new instructor. This is Mrs Kay who you know as your night guard.

Beat. None of the GIRLS *look up.*

Good. She will be here on Fridays for half an hour to give you some religious instruction. [*Pause.*] Right. File out.

The GIRLS *file off stage.*

MRS KAY: They didn't look at me.

NAYLOR: We might finally be getting somewhere.

MRS KAY: How do you mean?

NAYLOR: We still do get the odd one who continues to rebel, but I pride myself that there has been a margin of improvement.

MRS KAY: They're not allowed to look up?

NAYLOR looks at her and exits.

◆ ◆ ◆ ◆ ◆

SCENE SEVEN

The GIRLS *enter, marching. They stand at attention in front of their cells. They take three paces into their cells.*

MRS KAY: Lights out.

After a moment, from one of the cells, there is the sound of a girl crying. After a few moments another girl begins to softly join her. Then after another time there is a third girl crying.

MRS KAY listens. She stands to say something and then decides against it. Instead she begins to sing.

[*Singing*] In Dublin's fair city
Where the girls are so pretty
I first laid my eyes on sweet Molly Malone.
As she wheeled her wheelbarrow
Through the streets broad and narrow.
Crying cockles and mussels alive, alive, oh.
Alive alive oh, alive alive oh,
crying cockles and mussels alive, alive oh.

She was a fishmonger
And sure t'was no wonder
For so was her father and mother before
And they all wheeled their wheelbarrows
Through the streets broad and narrow
Crying cockles and mussels alive, alive, oh.
Alive alive oh, alive alive oh,
Crying cockles and mussels
Alive, alive oh.
She died of a fever
And no-one could save her
And that was the end of sweet Molly Malone
Now her ghost wheels that barrow
Through the streets broad and narrow
Crying cockles and mussels, alive, alive oh.
Alive alive oh, alive alive oh,
Crying cockles and mussels
Alive, alive oh.

There is silence after she finishes singing. The crying has stopped and the GIRLS *have got out of bed and come to the bars of their cells.*

EMMA: What was that?
MRS KAY: Well, it's a song.
MARJORIE: What's it called?
MRS KAY: It's called Molly Malone.
DANIELLA: My moth is called Molly.
MRS KAY: Do you know that song?
DANIELLA: No. I just called it that.
MRS KAY: That's nice.
DANIELLA: It's dead. Like Molly Malone. And when it died it must have known it was about to die because its wings are kind of folded back, all neatly and its legs are all folded forward all neatly. It must have known it was going to die, don't you think, like Molly knew when she got her fever.
MRS KAY: Get back into bed now girls.
MARJORIE: How do you know that song?
MRS KAY: Everyone knows that song. It's a folk song.

EMMA: From where?
MRS KAY: From Ireland.
MARJORIE: Is that where you're from?
MRS KAY: Yes. Now go back to bed girls or there'll be no more songs.
    The GIRLS *go back to bed. There is a silence.*
DANIELLA: Alive, alive oh.
MARJORIE: Alive, alive oh.
GIRLS: Crying cockles and mussels alive, alive oh.
    FIONA *walks forward, she is shivering. The other* GIRLS *circle her, they hold a thin blanket wrapped around their shoulders and then, in unison, begin to flap the sides of the blanket as if they are a flock of birds. They begin to caw and twitter like birds as they fly around then off and away, crumpled in a heap to sleep.*
FIONA: I am freezing to death
And wish that I could sleep.
The shivering of my shoulders shakes me,
breaks me.
Between sunup and sundown there is work
Repetitive, exhausting work
And there is
blank
rank
Silence.
My brain is whirring with it
My throat is dry
How monotonous is the loneliness of lips
The whispered intimacies of personal talk
How I long to chat and laugh
To talk
To form and roll words along my tongue
But there is only the cold
With claws that bite at my palms and feet.
Only the cold speaks
a varied language
of ruthless chill
of probing pain

I cannot rest
I cannot sleep
The shaking increases
I mutter to myself
I start at a and say
all the words
all the verbs
My teeth are chattering with adjectives,
unused.

♦ ♦ ♦ ♦ ♦

SCENE EIGHT

MARJORIE *walks onto the stage. She has a ping pong ball and bat and she hits the ball onto the side of the stage. The ball may be attached by string to the bat.*

MARJORIE: With all this looking at the floor, I had a dream.

> EMMA *enters. She also has a ping pong ball and bat and hits it onto the floor of the stage.*

EMMA: With all this looking at the floor, I had a dream about ping pong.

> GWEN *enters. She also has a ping pong ball and hits it onto the floor of the stage.*

GWEN: With all this looking at the floor I had a dream about ping pong balls.

> FIONA *enters. She also has a ping pong ball and hits it onto the floor of the stage.*

FIONA: With all this looking at the floor I had a dream about ping pong balls and how they bounce.

> DANIELLA *enters. She also has a ping pong ball and hits it on the floor.*

DANIELLA: With all this looking at the floor I had a dream about ping pong balls and how they bounce out of my head.

MARJORIE: I dreamt they were like my eyes.

EMMA: With all this staring at the floor.

GWEN: Seeing shoes, seeing dirt, seeing concrete.

FIONA: I dreamt that all of the officers surrounded me.
DANIELLA: And then they held me down and started gouging at my eyes.

> *The* GIRLS *all hold* MARJORIE *down and there is a struggle. One of the ping pong balls flies across the stage and rolls. There is more of a struggle and another of the balls flies out and rolls.*

> MARJORIE *emerges, she has her eyes closed. Black may have been put on the eye area, making it look like her eyes have popped out. Fake blood is optional.*

MARJORIE: And in the dream I was laughing.
GWEN: Laughing.
EMMA: Because at first it was funny.
FIONA: With all this looking at the floor.
DANIELLA: I lost my eyesight.

> MARJORIE *drops to the floor, blindly searching for the balls, crawling on her hands and knees and then, successively, so do all the others.*

MARJORIE: With all this looking at the floor I had a dream.
GWEN: With all this looking at the floor I had a dream that I searched and searched.
EMMA: With all this looking at the floor I had a dream that I searched and searched but I couldn't find my eyes.
FIONA: With all this looking at the floor I had a dream that I searched and searched but I couldn't find my eyes and I imagined them covered in all the filth of the floor.
DANIELLA: With all this looking at the floor I had a dream that I searched and searched but I couldn't find my eyes and I imagined them covered in the filth of the floor ...
GIRLS: ... and I wasn't laughing anymore.

♦ ♦ ♦ ♦ ♦

SCENE NINE

NAYLOR *comes in carrying a hay bale. He walks to the centre of the stage where he puts down the bale then climbs on top of it. All the* GIRLS *sit in a semicircle underneath it. He pulls a pair of garden shears from his pocket and begins to cut the hay, so that bits and pieces of it fall down over the* GIRLS *sitting underneath.*

NAYLOR: We don't cut their hair because we are barbaric. We don't like having to cut off their hair. I'd go so far as to say that we don't even like having them here. But we didn't ask them to be here. They are uncontrollable, rebellious girls. I know there may be reasons why they are like that. I know that many of them have had very hard childhoods. But that does not discount that fact that now, now, our society is having to deal with them and they are, dreadful. Really dreadful girls. Perhaps any ladylike behaviour has been beaten out of them or bullied out of them. But however it has been removed it is doubtless gone from them. You can't reason with them. And in your heart of hearts you know that I am right. There are girls like this. There are girls who, perhaps for no fault of their own, or perhaps simply because they choose not to learn from their mistakes, are wild, hostile, barbaric little wild animals. And they must be corrected. They must be corrected. And that is why we cut off their hair. And it's not barbaric. It's not cruel and indifferent. Hair will grow back. But they need to learn to submit. Goodness I submit. There's a lot of things I have to do that I don't like doing. There's a lot of things in life that you just have to force yourself to submit to. But these girls won't accept that. They smash things, they bite each other, they hurt themselves. I'm not making this up. Maybe you think that they aren't so bad. Well I do this day in and day out and I'm here to tell you that these are wild little bitches who need to have everything taken from them before they are prepared to listen. Well fine. If you're not going to listen we are going to take you down. We are going to take everything away from you until you do listen.

He holds the scissors up into the air.
Next.

◆ ◆ ◆ ◆ ◆

SCENE TEN

NAYLOR *and* JANE.

NAYLOR: Jane?

JANE: Yes, sir.
NAYLOR: That is your name.
JANE: Yes, sir.
NAYLOR: Yes. However we have another Jane arriving.
JANE: Yes, sir.
NAYLOR: So that will be a problem for us.
JANE: A problem, sir?
NAYLOR: Two girls with the same name.
JANE: Sir.
NAYLOR: We can't have that.
JANE: Am I being sent back to Parramatta?
NAYLOR: No.
JANE: Will you call us by our surnames, sir?
NAYLOR: We could do that.
JANE: Yes, sir.
NAYLOR: But I don't think that will work for us.
JANE: Sir?
NAYLOR: There is only one solution.
JANE: Yes, sir.
NAYLOR: You see what we have to do don't you, Jane?
JANE: I'm not … I don't …
NAYLOR: Brain engaged, girl.
JANE: You'll call us by our numbers, sir?
NAYLOR: No. Call you by your numbers? What do you think we are?
JANE: Then …
NAYLOR: Think child. Honestly, the stupidity of you girls is exhausting. Sometimes I think that you don't have brains at all, only useless grey mush.
JANE: Not our surname …
NAYLOR: Yes.
JANE: Not our number …
NAYLOR: Yes.
JANE: Not sent away …
NAYLOR: And …
JANE: Not able to have two of us.
NAYLOR: Logic child? Use a bit of logic can you?
JANE: You wouldn't?
NAYLOR: Wouldn't what?

JANE: No, please, sir please don't.
NAYLOR: Please don't what?
JANE: Please don't ... kill me.
> *Pause. He slaps her. He kicks her. He punches her.*

NAYLOR: You are a stupid, worthless, worthless piece of rubbish.
JANE: I'm sorry sir.
NAYLOR: I'd like to kill you, because of your utter idiocy. Kill you! Get back to your dorm, right this minute.
> JANE *begins to leave.*

Wait.
> JANE *stops.*

NAYLOR: You will be called Joanne.
JANE: Sir?
NAYLOR: We will call the new girl Jane and you will be Joanne. You will answer to Joanne when an officer addresses you as such.
JANE: Joanne?
NAYLOR: Yes, Joanne.
JANE: But ...
NAYLOR: But what, Joanne?
JANE: My name is Jane.
NAYLOR: Your name is Joanne.
JANE: But why?
NAYLOR: Because I say it is.
> *Pause.*

NAYLOR: Did you think that your name was something that belonged to you? Did you think that your name was the only thing that no-one could take away from you? Did you?
> JANE *nods.*

[*Amused*] I killed Jane off.
JANE: But I am Jane.
NAYLOR: If we had any sense I would rename all of you. Give you all a fresh start. But as it transpires only you will be lucky enough to have that done for you.
JANE: I am Jane.
NAYLOR: You are nothing. [*Beat.*] Now get out.

◆ ◆ ◆ ◆ ◆

SCENE ELEVEN

DANIELLA *is lying in bed, speaking aloud. Two other actors appear, upstage, and act out the scene she is describing, as the spider and the fly. They may have cups from the dining room scene or other props on their eyes.*

DANIELLA: Bzzzz.
Bzzzzz.
Bzzzz.
It's on the roof of my cell.
A fly has been caught by a spider. The web has probably only snared its leg or its wing, only one small part of it. But that's enough. The spider is alerted to its catch by the desperate tugging on the threads of its trap and also by a low, mournful buzzing.
Bzzzzz.
Bzzzzz.
Bzzzzz.
The spider crawls towards its catch. I can't quite see but it looks like it goes in and bites it on the head, or something like that. The fly is still buzzing but the action of the wings is getting lower. The buzzing is no longer a desperate struggling zzzzz but a continuous moaning bzzzzt, bzzzzt. The spider becomes a dancer, it is wrapping up the fly in long threads of web. Around and around and around it dances, and then it falls back, like a maniac weaver, and tugs the threads tight across the body of the fly. The buzzing continues and continues.
Bzzzzt.
Bzzzzzt.
Bzzzzt.
I can see other flies on the walls. They are still. They are silent. The spider dances again like some insane grandmother with lethal crochet hooks, conducting the air with sticky fibres. Bzzzzt.
Bzzzzt.
Bzzzzt.
Long after it knows its fate. Long after it is wrapped and tied. Long after the spider advances toward it to suck it dry.
When I look up in the morning there will be a small little husk. Or

it will have fallen to the floor where I will find it. I will get into trouble if I leave the cobwebs hanging in my cell until they can be seen. But I don't care. I am in league with the spider. I am in league. I love to watch him feeding.

♦♦♦♦♦

SCENE TWELVE

The GIRLS *march on stage. They sit around in a circle. They all hold bras. The first* GIRL *cuts off the hooks and eyes on the bra. She then passes the scissors to the next* GIRL *who also proceeds to unpick the hooks and eyes. When the* GIRL *has taken them off she hands them to* FUREDI *who is waiting for them. At one point* FUREDI *goes over to get some buttons which he gives to the first* GIRL. *The* GIRL *then begins to sew the buttons on.* FUREDI *proceeds down the row to each* GIRL *getting hooks and eyes and giving out buttons. Suddenly he notices that something is wrong.*

FUREDI: Where is the other piece?

    MARJORIE *looks at the ground.*

Marjorie Linnett. Where is the hook from this bra?

    MARJORIE *looks at the ground.*

No girl will leave here until you hand over the hook from this bra.

    MARJORIE *still says nothing.*

Get up.

    MARJORIE *stands.*

Give me the hook, immediately.

    MARJORIE *looks at the ground.* FUREDI *hits her on the legs at the end of every sentence.*

Why do you think we have to get you to do this? Because we know what you'll do with little pieces of wire. What did you do in Parramatta? Do you think I don't know that you swallowed them? Do you think I don't know that you cut yourself with them? Why do you think that we make you sew on these buttons?

    MARJORIE *falls to her knees.*

Now where is that hook?

> MARJORIE *sticks out her tongue and the hook is on it.* FUREDI *puts out his hand.* MARJORIE *spits the hook slowly into* FUREDI*'s hand.* FUREDI *slaps* MARJORIE *with his right hand and knocks her to the ground.*

Carry on.

♦ ♦ ♦ ♦ ♦

SCENE THIRTEEN

Through their cell flap, JANE *and* DANIELLA *are comparing their legs and arms. They speak in barely a whisper.*

JANE: See my arms are just that little bit longer than yours.
DANIELLA: Yeah, but you're older than me.
JANE: No, it's more than that. Show us your legs.

They compare the length of their legs.

See that's another sign.
DANIELLA: No it's not.
JANE: Yeah, it is. Now stick out your tongue. [*She sticks her own tongue out.*] How far can you stick your tongue out?

They both stick their tongues out.

Yeah, see that's another sign.
DANIELLA: Of what?
JANE: Of that you're more tainted than me.
DANIELLA: How come?
JANE: No, it's nothing you did. It's just the way you are.
DANIELLA: I'm not.
JANE: Yeah, you are. For sure, you're more tainted than me.
DANIELLA: What's that?
JANE: Tainted stock. I heard one of them, MacPherson, explaining it.
DANIELLA: And can you change it?
JANE: No, you just are it. You just have it in your blood that makes you bad.
DANIELLA: Yeah?
JANE: Yeah. You're just tainted and you need to be kept away from the untainted.

DANIELLA: How come?
JANE: I dunno. So that you don't, you know, taint them up or something.
DANIELLA: Right.
JANE: Can you get your hand around your head?

They both put their arms around the back of their heads.

JANE: Yeah, see, that's another sign of you're more tainted than me.
DANIELLA: I don't want to be more tainted.
JANE: I know but you can't get out of it. You're just bad.
DANIELLA: I'm not bad.
JANE: Yeah, you are. You're just bad and the only thing you understand is isolation and punishment. And no matter what you do that's just how you'll always be. How far is it from your chin to your ear?

They measure with their hands.

DANIELLA: Hey, Fiona.
FIONA: Shut up, Daniella.

DANIELLA *mumbles something with her mouth closed.*

What are you doing?
DANIELLA: I'm shutting up, but I've got to tell you.
FIONA: You're such a retard.
DANIELLA: I know. But so are you.
FIONA: I'm what?
JANE: You're tainted.
FIONA: Says who?
JANE: You can measure it.
DANIELLA: Yeah, you can measure your leg. Like this.
FIONA: Shut up, retard.
JANE: That's the taint coming out.
FIONA: Yeah. Just you remember that.

The GIRLS *open their eyes and mouths wide as if in shock and then take a breath and pretend to be swimming underwater, holding their breaths. They do breast stroke toward the audience and then other styles of swimming, as* FIONA *speaks.*

It is boiling hot
And we cannot sleep
Inside our tiny cells
is airless

prayerless
Mrs Kay takes her children to the local pool
Said she felt mean
But here too there is
dripping
slipping
water.
My arms are thick with it
My neck runs rivers
My hair is damp
How delicious would be an immersion in water
the silk of sliding strokes
How I long to dive and paddle
in the satin of shimmering water
Of fluidity, of liquid
Of melt
But we may not go to the pool
We may not leave our cells
I stand on my bed to get closer to the night
The crickets scratching dryness
I cannot rest
I cannot sleep
The sweat glands churn like oceans
Making patches on the mattress
Making patterns on my nightwear
I dip my finger in the ink of my own excretions
And draw pictures of children swimming
Onto the dusty walls.

♦ ♦ ♦ ♦ ♦

SCENE FOURTEEN

MARJORIE *is in solitary confinement.* FUREDI *enters and puts down a tray with bread and water. The other actors enter and they behave like clocks, their hands all ticking forward and all ticking together. They seem to tick slowly and then stop altogether, which makes* MARJORIE *get up and try to get them started again, but instead they start ticking backwards. One of the 'clocks' turns into* MARJORIE'S FATHER *(double for* NAYLOR*). He holds a mini-skirt.*

FATHER: You're not wearing this to the wedding.
MARJORIE: Too much?
FATHER: Don't get smart with me.
MARJORIE: Or what?
FATHER: Or you'll find out.
MARJORIE: You've already stopped me from going out on Friday night, going out on a Saturday night with every other kid from school.
FATHER: I don't want you going to those places.
MARJORIE: You mean places where I might have fun, Dad?
FATHER: You could have fun at the wedding if you put your mind to it.
MARJORIE: The whole room will be chocka with wrinklies.
FATHER: Don't speak about my friends like that.
MARJORIE: Or what?

The clocks turn again.

One of the 'clocks' turns into MARJORIE'S FRIEND. *She starts to dance with her.*

FRIEND: Come do the cha-cha-cha at Ourimbah!
MARJORIE: He said I can't go.
FRIEND: We'll drink Coo-la-ba and laugh ha ha ha at the pop festival at Ourimbah.
MARJORIE: He'll kill me if I don't go to this stupid wedding.
FRIEND: There'll be boys cha cha, who'll slip off your bra, and you'll go ooh-la-la at Ourimbah.
MARJORIE: It's not fair that I can't go.
FRIEND: So just come with us.
MARJORIE: He never let's me do anything. He's virtually locked me up and thrown away the key since mum died.
FRIEND: So come.
MARJORIE: Run away?
FRIEND Come on. It's going to be the biggest pop music festival of the year. You've got to be there.
MARJORIE: I'll do it.
FRIEND: Come on. What can he do to you?

The FRIEND *steps back and becomes a 'clock' again. All of the clocks seem to 'melt' and dance and groove to the pop music sounds. Then suddenly they become clocks again, ticking fast and sort of breathing heavily.* MARJORIE *is with* LENNY.

LENNY: Which of your senses is the most heightened?
MARJORIE: Um, I dunno. Sound?
LENNY: Yeah. The sound of another human being right in close to you. The sound of you whispering, the smallest crackle of your breath, the tiniest tap of your teeth.
MARJORIE: That sounds nice.
LENNY: The sound of the music and the crowds and the mud and the music.
MARJORIE: The sound of the night and the outdoors and the dark.
LENNY: My hearing has become incredibly sensitised. I feel like I can hear for miles.
MARJORIE: Kilometres even.
LENNY: Yes.
MARJORIE: 'Cause a major part of attraction is people's voice rather than their looks.
LENNY: You don't like how I look?
MARJORIE: I haven't seen all of you yet.
LENNY: Just say the words.
MARJORIE: Kiss me?

She leans to kiss him but as she does the clocks sound like a clock alarm.

Two of the clocks become police officers and grab MARJORIE.

OFFICER 1: Come with us.
MARJORIE: What are you doing?
OFFICER 2: Don't make this harder than it has to be.
MARJORIE: Make what harder?
OFFICER 1: Your father reported you missing.
MARJORIE: So just let me go home.
OFFICER 2: You're not going home.
MARJORIE: What?
OFFICER 1: You're being charged.
MARJORIE: I haven't done anything wrong.
OFFICER 2: No, you're not going to be punished.
MARJORIE: I want to go home.

OFFICER 1: You've been exposed to moral danger.
MARJORIE: I … can I see my father?
OFFICER 2: You'll see him in court.
MARJORIE: In court?
OFFICER 1: It's for your protection. For your own protection.
MARJORIE: What is?

The 'clocks' return to their original position and tick slowly.

MARJORIE *sits, staring at them.*

SCENE FIFTEEN

EMMA *and* GWEN *are in a solitary confinement cell. They are marked with bruises all over their bodies and have obviously been viciously bashed.* EMMA *looks up at the ceiling.*

EMMA: Look at that.
GWEN: What?
EMMA: I can see the stars.

GWEN *looks at her.*

GWEN: Don't go weird on me, squirt.
EMMA: I'm not. Look again.
GWEN: What's up there is the roof, runt. The concrete roof.
EMMA: Yes, but outside the roof is the stars. Is really the stars.
GWEN: Yeah, right.
EMMA: If there was no roof we would be able to see the stars.
GWEN: Pity about the roof then.

Pause.

EMMA: The roof is boring. I'd rather look at the stars.

She lays down on the floor of the cell and looks up.

Come on.

GWEN *doesn't move.*

Come on, Sis.
GWEN: Don't call me that.
EMMA: Come on then.

GWEN *lays down. They both look up at the ceiling.*

GWEN: You could see more in Cootamundra.
EMMA: You could see even more at Carowa.
GWEN: Yeah.
EMMA: I bet if we ever got back to Carowa, you'd remember it.
GWEN: Just look at the stars will ya.
EMMA: You would. You'd remember the stars and you'd remember Dad. And you'd remember me, Sis.
GWEN: I told you not to call me that.
EMMA: But you are. I know you are.
GWEN: You don't know I am.
EMMA: But you look just like me.
GWEN: You reckon.
EMMA: I can tell that you are.
GWEN: Yeah.

Pause.

What was home like?
EMMA: My home? Carowa?
GWEN: Yeah?
EMMA: Pretty dry. There was one big tree, that you was born under.
GWEN: What is it like?
EMMA: Big. Lots of shade. That's where your mother had ya.
GWEN: Why under the tree?
EMMA: Dunno. That's just what they used to tell me. That my sister was born under the the big tree with lots of shade. And that's why they called her Penny. Because the shade under that tree was like a big brown penny all around your mother the whole time she was giving birth.
GWEN: But my name isn't Penny.
EMMA: They does that all the time. If they took ya away they mixed up your names so you couldn't find your way back. But I'm smarter than they are. Because Gwennie is like Pennie. They changed your name but only a little. They didn't want me to know you because it was my father with your mother and not my mother. But your mother told me about you.

GWEN *sits up and looks at her, long and hard.*

EMMA: One day the memories will come back. They will. And I'll be here to help them come. I'll be right next to you. I will.

    EMMA *lays back down and looks at the roof.*

♦♦♦♦♦

SCENE SIXTEEN

The GIRLS *line up for Religious Instruction Class. They stand in a line with their eyes to the floor.* MRS KAY *enters.*

MRS KAY: Good morning, girls.
GIRLS: Good morning, Mrs Kay.
    They continue to stand.
MRS KAY: Oh. Oh. Permission to be seated.
    The GIRLS *all sit.*

Good, now first. During religious instruction class you will not be required to keep your eyes on the ground.
    The GIRLS *continue to look at the ground.*
I repeat, you will not be required to keep your eyes to the ground.
    The GIRLS *continue to look at the ground.*
Girls, eyes to the front.
    The GIRLS *continue to look at the ground.*
JANE: That's been used as a trick on us before.
MRS KAY: I beg your pardon?
JANE: That's been used as a trick on us before. Where we've been told we can look up and then corrected when we do.
MRS KAY: [*sighing*] This is not a trick. Girls, I would like you to look up at me when I read the lesson and then for the duration of the class.
    The GIRLS *still do not look up.*
Today's reading is from Colossians Chapter 2 verses 18 to 25. Wives, be committed to your husbands, as is fitting in Christ. Husbands love your wives and never treat them harshly. Children, heed your parents in everything, for this is your acceptable duty

in Christ. Parents, do not provoke your children, or they may lose heart. You who are enslaved, heed your earthly masters in everything, not only while being watched and in order to please them, but wholeheartedly, revering the Lord. Whatever your task, put yourselves into it, as done for the Lord and not for human beings, since you know that from the Lord you will receive the inheritance as your reward; you serve the Lord Christ. For the wrongdoer will be paid back for whatever wrong has been done, and there is no partiality.

The GIRLS *are still not looking up.*

Does anyone have any questions? Or comments?

The GIRLS *still do not look up.*

Will you look at me, please. Girls.

Pause. The GIRLS *continue to look at the floor. But then,* FIONA *puts up her hand.*

FIONA: What does it mean, never treat them harshly?

MRS KAY: I won't answer unless you look at me, Fiona.

FIONA *very slowly, very hesitantly, looks up at* MRS KAY.

MRS KAY: Thank you. [*Beat.*] Now you may repeat your question.

FIONA: Husbands, love your wives and never treat them badly. What does that mean?

MRS KAY: What do you think it means?

FIONA: I don't know. That's why I asked.

MRS KAY: Anyone else?

Pause.

GWEN: It means they should stop before they beat their brains out.

MRS KAY: It does mean that. It means, of course, that they should not be beaten.

JANE: What never?

MRS KAY: No. Never.

DANIELLA: Not even if they deserve it.

MRS KAY: No-one ever deserves to be treated in a violent manner.

JANE: What is a violent manner?

MARJORIE: It's when you grab someone around the neck and you slam them into a door frame over and over and over again until they're like bleeding from the head and from the nose and from the mouth.

That means you shouldn't do that.
   Pause.
MRS KAY: Marjorie is quite right.
EMMA: Are we enslaved?
MRS KAY: I beg your pardon?
EMMA: Like it says, you who are enslaved. I'm just trying to work out if we are enslaved.
GWEN: Shut up, Emma.
EMMA: I was only asking.
MRS KAY: No you are not enslaved.
EMMA: I wasn't saying we were. I was just asking if we were.
GWEN: Shut up, Emma.
MRS KAY: She is entitled to ask.
GWEN: And you're entitled to mention it to the Superintendent.
MRS KAY: I promise not to do that.
GWEN: What?
MRS KAY: If you have questions about the scriptures I will not be mentioning them to the Superintendent.
   Pause.
Any other questions?
FIONA: When it says the wrongdoer will be paid back for whatever wrong has been done ... ?
MRS KAY: Paid back by God.
FIONA: When?
MRS KAY: Well, when we face our maker.
JANE: Is that like the judge we faced in the Children's Court?
MRS KAY: A little like that.
JANE: So we can get blamed for other wrongdoers' actions?
MRS KAY: No, you will only have to face God and reveal your own wrongdoings.
DANIELLA: But in the children's court we can be charged with being neglected and we can be charged with being exposed to moral danger.
MRS KAY: Yes. Those are particular circumstances.
   Pause.
FIONA: What about if someone else did wrong to you first?
MRS KAY: Then they will have to face God and explain it.

FIONA: Will they really?

MRS KAY: Yes. What kind of wrongdoing are you thinking of?

GWEN: Don't answer her.

MRS KAY: I beg your pardon, Gwen?

GWEN: She imagines things, Miss, that's all. She imagines things and I wouldn't want her to worry you with the kinds of things she imagines. We're used to them now but since you don't know her you might take her seriously and that would just worry you. You know.

MRS KAY: I think I can make up my own mind about whether or not she is imagining things, don't you Gwen.

GWEN: She's really clever. She tells a story and you know, sometimes I even believe her.

MRS KAY: Stories about what?

GWEN *glares are* FIONA.

Fiona?

FIONA: I don't have any stories today, Miss. I just liked the idea of God sitting up like in the judges box and judging everyone.

MRS KAY: Yes. In the end we will all be called to account.

FIONA: Only sometimes judges get it wrong.

GWEN *glares at* FIONA *again.*

I mean, not any judges we know. But you hear about them. Judges on other planets you know. Judges on Mars and Venus and all the way out on Pluto.

GWEN *puts a hand around her ear like* FIONA *is cuckoo.* MRS KAY *looks at them but they all have their eyes back to the ground.*

◆ ◆ ◆ ◆ ◆

SCENE SEVENTEEN

SUPERINTENDENT NAYLOR *enters.*

NAYLOR: Extract from the Riverine Grazier, 3 May 1962.

As NAYLOR *reads, the* GIRLS *begin to to do their work on stage. They scrub the floors in a pair, they garden with a spade in a pair and with a trowel in a pair.*

The headline reads, Hay Girls Home a credit to Welfare Department.

HAWKINS: The Institution for Girls conducted by the Department of Child Welfare and Social Welfare is a small institution but has already demonstrated a significant role in the total programme of child welfare.

NAYLOR: Said the Minister in charge of that Department, the Hon F. H. Hawkins when in Hay in February.

The GIRLS *continue to work.*

HAWKINS: The press will understand that this is a closed institution but in the autumn, when the flower gardens are in full bloom, the Grazier will be permitted to see the transformation which is taking place.

NAYLOR: The pictures on this page are the result.

The GIRLS *get up from their work and begin to behave like flowers, their hands out as if in bloom, their faces smiling. A small red paper flower may emerge from their hands. But they hold the smile too long and the smile appears fixed and horrible.*

Each girl picks two bunches of flowers each week from their own gardens for her own room.

The GIRLS, *still behaving like flowers, begin to wither and die. They hang limply and fall to the ground where they begin to scrub and dig again.*

As one enters through the large blue door, the immediate view is of spacious green lawns, bisected with spotlessly clean cement paths, with garden plots surrounding all the buildings.

The GIRLS *again get up from their work and 'bloom' like flowers, the fixed smiles on their faces. But the poses they take are less easy, instead their limbs are twisted and their stances are awkward.*

Their duties include bed making, sweeping and the arrangement of flowers.

The GIRLS *fade again, wilting and dying as they go to the ground to do their work.*

Very old residents of Hay will remember this property when it was occupied with male civil prisoners and used to take many prizes at the flower shows of the day.

The GIRLS *'bloom' as flowers again, but their limbs are as tangled as they can possibly make them, their heads on a strange angle, even though they are smiling and their stances almost impossible to hold for very long without collapsing, which they do at the limits of their endurance.*

Those with shorter memories have only a picture of a derelict building and untidy grounds that no-one would touch for any sort of purpose.

The GIRLS *stand at attention, their eyes to the floor.*

Now the place has been restored in an almost unbelievable way and shows just what can be done when interested people set out to restore order and grow gardens.

The GIRLS *bob down and roll themselves into as small a ball as possible.* MRS KAY *speaks to the audience.*

MRS KAY: Maybe you've seen the picture, in the Riverine Grazier, showing the basic cells. They mostly slept well, after their hard work on the concrete paths. They had a couple of rough grey blankets each. It was enough but you wouldn't say they were really cosy, because the cells were freezing, the whole block was freezing. And their beds had to be made exactly so, like in the army. They had to be out from the wall at a slight angle, so that you could see the girls asleep at night. They were allowed two items on their bed tables. Those flowers in the photo were only put in their for effect. They weren't allowed flowers.

MRS KAY *exits.* FUREDI *remains on stage.*

♦ ♦ ♦ ♦ ♦

SCENE EIGHTEEN

The GIRLS *stand across the front of the stage. They all have glasses of water and* DANIELLA, *at the end, has a jug. The girl closest to* DANIELLA *pours her glass of water into* DANIELLA*'s jug.* DANIELLA *puts her hand up, as is required of her.*

DANIELLA: Permission to go to the toilet, sir. [*Beat.*] Try to think about something else. A tree. A tall tree. White trunk. Green leaves. A gum tree. Wind in the leaves. Pale green leaves with white undersides. Bending, swaying. A clear blue sky.

The girl next to the the girl alongside DANIELLA *pours her glass of water carefully into the glass of the girl alongside* DANIELLA *who then pours that into the jug of water* DANIELLA *is holding.*

[*With more urgency*] Permission to go to the toilet, please, sir. A great dry plain. Yellow grass. Fields of long white yellow grass. Bone dry. The ground cracking it is so dry. Spinifex rolling. Dried out clumps of spinifex grass tumbling and rolling across the dry, windy landscape. Cartwheellng and tumbling completely free. Blown by the wind. The wind in the tree.

The girl third in line pours the water into the glass of the next girl, who pours it into the glass of the girl next to DANIELLA, *who pours it in to the jug which is now close to the top.*

Miss, permission please please, I have to go to the toilet. I have to go. I'm begging you to go. [*Beat.*] The caves up behind the house. The red of the rock, the pale dry whiteness of the sand in the red rock cave. The view out to the great dry plain. The spinifex skipping and twirling. The gum tree swaying and bending. The sun glinting on the breeze on the leaves. A glorious day. A glorious sunny day, safe and happy and smiling and O God, O God please let me go to the toilet. Please I have to go to the toilet. Please give me permission. Please.

The fourth girl in line pours the glass of water and it passes down the line until it gets to DANIELLA's *jug where it starts to overflow. The girl continues pouring till the water runs down* DANIELLA's *arm and keeps pouring down the side of her body, along her trousers and to the ground in a small puddle.*

[*Crying*] The pretty little stream at the base of the cliff. The pretty little stream running past the white trunk green leaf gum tree swaying in the wind. The delicate stream running past the yellow grass and the rolling spinifex. The gentle pretty stream flowing past the red rock cave, the shining sunny day. The pretty, flowing stream, sparkling in the daylight.

DANIELLA *exits.*

SCENE NINETEEN

The GIRLS *all stand in line with pieces of painted 'wall' in front of them (the 'wall' may be solid paint at the first piece and then brick by the end of the row).* FIONA *has a scrubbing brush and a bucket of water and she scrubs on the 'wall'.*

FIONA: When you first start you can't believe that it isn't just paint all the way down. That there isn't really any brick under all those layers. But there is and you just have to scrub and scrub and scrub until you get to it.

She scrubs at each successive piece of 'wall' and when she can scrub no more the the performer lowers it to the ground so that only her arms are visible over the top of the 'wall', holding a scrubbing brush.

FIONA *continues to scrub.*

♦ ♦ ♦ ♦ ♦

SCENE TWENTY

MARJORIE *and* MR NAYLOR *are in* NAYLOR's *office.* MARJORIE *is standing at attention, eyes to the floor,* NAYLOR *sits in a chair at his desk.*

NAYLOR: You know why you're here, Linnett.
MARJORIE: No, Mr Naylor.
NAYLOR: Yes, you do. Why are you here?
MARJORIE: I don't know, Mr Naylor.
NAYLOR: Don't contradict me.

Pause.

Why are you here?

MARJORIE *says nothing.*

Let me give you a hint. It has something to do with your face.

MARJORIE *still says nothing.*

Tell me what people say about your face.

MARJORIE *says nothing.*

I said, tell me.

MARJORIE: My mother used to say that it resembles nothing so much as a slapped arse.

NAYLOR: That is what your mother said to you is it?

MARJORIE: Yes, Mr Naylor.

NAYLOR: She set you a poor example.

Pause.

Has anyone in here spoken to you about your face?

MARJORIE *says nothing.*

Answer me.

MARJORIE: The guards have said about my eyebrows but I've told them that they just grow like that.

NAYLOR *gets up and walks around the office.*

NAYLOR: They just grow like that?

MARJORIE: Yes, Mr Naylor.

NAYLOR: You don't pluck them at night?

MARJORIE: No, Mr Naylor.

Pause.

NAYLOR: You think that your eyebrows give you a certain distinction.

MARJORIE: No, Mr Naylor.

NAYLOR: Of course you do, you think that they give you personality.

MARJORIE: I'm sure I don't, Mr Naylor.

NAYLOR: Your contradictions don't irritate me, Linnett. They make me pity you.

Pause.

Why? Because they reveal how very very stupid you really are.

MARJORIE *shifts where she is standing.*

You pluck your eyebrows, Linnett. You do it at night in your cell, with your fingernails because you think it gives you control. I would go so far as to say that you think that your eyebrows give you individuality because, due to the mismanagement of your mother and the delinquency of your own nature, you think that individuality is something to have. Don't you, Linnett?

MARJORIE: No, Mr Naylor.

NAYLOR: Yes, you do. But you're lucky because I'm going to teach you something that will help you. You won't thank me for it. I'm not looking for thanks. What I'm going to teach you, Linnett, is that you are nothing. That the very best of us, the very best of us are nothing. We have no individuality, we have no personality. We are servants. We are nothing.

MARJORIE: Yes, Mr Naylor.

NAYLOR: Do you think that life in this institution is hard, Linnett?

MARJORIE: No, Mr Naylor.

> NAYLOR *goes over to her and, as casually as if he is hitting a fly, slaps her hard across the head.*

Do you think that life in this institution is hard, Linnett?

MARJORIE: Yes, Mr Naylor.

NAYLOR: Yes, it is hard. Why?

MARJORIE: I don't know, Mr Naylor.

> NAYLOR *hits her again.*

NAYLOR: What are you, Linnett?

MARJORIE: I'm nothing, Mr Naylor.

NAYLOR: You're nothing, but, and remember this Linnett, I'm also nothing. Being nothing is not about what you're worth, Linnett. It is true that you are worth nothing because your family are poor, if you don't kill yourself with drugs and alcohol you will certainly have children at an early age. You are worth nothing. And yet we are taking the trouble to correct you. If you go missing from this institution we will not send anyone out to find you, however. Why? Because you are worth nothing. You could starve out there, die out there and we would do little more than go through the motions of finding you. Why? Because you are worth nothing. The only time you will begin to be worth something is when you become nothing. When you learn to deny yourself and discipline yourself and push through. You are nothing because you are worth nothing. I am nothing because I choose to be nothing other than discipline and service and self-control. And by embracing nothingness I have become something, something and someone. Do you want to be that, Linnett?

MARJORIE: Do I want to be you, Mr Naylor?

NAYLOR: Yes, Linnett, do you want to serve your community in a way that they will be grateful for and reward you for?

MARJORIE: Yes, Mr Naylor.

> NAYLOR *goes over to her and knocks her to the ground. He slaps and kicks her.*

NAYLOR: Then stop plucking your eyebrows, Linnett.

MARJORIE: Yes, Mr Naylor.

> NAYLOR *grabs her up and looks her in the face.*

NAYLOR: If you don't, I will commit you to psychiatric treatment and from a place such as that you will never, never get out. Do you understand me?

> MARJORIE *nods.*

MARJORIE: Yes, Mr Naylor.

NAYLOR: What will you do, Linnett?

MARJORIE: I will stop plucking my eyebrows and become nothing, Mr Naylor.

> *He releases her.*

NAYLOR: See that you do.

♦ ♦ ♦ ♦ ♦

SCENE TWENTY-ONE

The GIRLS, *as a group, march into the cabin block where they stand in front of their cells and mark time.*

FUREDI: Halt.

> *The* GIRLS *stop marching.*

Left and right, turn.

> *The* GIRLS *turn one way or the other to face their cells.*

Two paces forward. March.

> *The* GIRLS *take two paces into their cells.*

Cans down.

> *The* GIRLS *put down their night pans.*

Two paces backwards, march.

> *The* GIRLS *march backwards.*

To your lockers, march.

The GIRLS *all troupe out one by one to go to their lockers and collect their change of clothing, tooth brush and comb.*

FUREDI *exits. Out of their lockers the* GIRLS *take cell bars, like batons, and begin dancing around them, cuddling them, running them over their bodies.*

FIONA: I am scared to death
And wish I could relax
I want to hurt someone
Like I have been held down
and ground down
and pierced.
I am corroded with fear
My veins ring with it
I flash on my past
The boys who ripped me
Stripped me
But that is no excuse
Fiona
You have betrayed yourself
Fiona
Take it back
Take back the mistake
Take back the error
Hide the thing or you will never leave
Hide the thing or you will not survive
Hide it
Hide yourself
Retreat and hide inside
Forever
Inside
And never show yourself again.

♦ ♦ ♦ ♦ ♦

SCENE TWENTY-TWO

GWEN *and* EMMA *are whispering.*

GWEN: There was a big old tree. And there was an old fella. White beard, dark hat. Black maybe brown. He had a gold cap on his front tooth. And he was saying to me thina. I remember he said thina, thina. Thina. Thina. Kiruu thina. Kiruu thina.
EMMA: And what was he doing?
GWEN: I don't know.
EMMA: Think.
> *Pause.*

GWEN: I think ... I'm not sure ... but I think he was touching my feet.
> *Pause.* EMMA *is overcome. Looking up at the ceiling to stop herself crying.*

EMMA: Warm toes.
GWEN: What?
EMMA: Kiruu thina. Warm toes. It would have been paapaa saying you had nice warm feet. Kiruu thina. Warm feet or warm toes in Ngiyampaa.
> GWEN *looks at* EMMA.

GWEN: What does that mean?
EMMA: That means you're a Barkindji woman. And you really are my sister.
> GWEN *and* EMMA *turn over their stainless steel buckets and begin drumming and the other* GIRLS *also take their buckets and drum on them.*

SCENE TWENTY-THREE

MARJORIE *and* DANIELLA *are breaking up the concrete path, outside their cells.*

DANIELLA: Marjorie.
MARJORIE: What?
DANIELLA: How did you go with Naylor?
MARJORIE: Told me to stop plucking my eyebrows.
DANIELLA: Or what?

MARJORIE: Or I'd go to the psych home.
> *Pause.*

DANIELLA: So you're going to, aren't ya?
MARJORIE: Maybe.
DANIELLA: You've got to.
MARJORIE: Yeah, I know. I can't help myself sometimes that's all.
DANIELLA: I know.
MARJORIE: No, ya don't.
DANIELLA: Yeah, I do. You get lonely. So you pluck your eyebrows.
> *Pause.*

I don't know what I'd do without Molly.
MARJORIE: Who?
DANIELLA: Little Molly Malone.
MARJORIE: You mean the song?
DANIELLA: No. I've got this moth.
MARJORIE: Can I see?

> DANIELLA *takes out Molly Malone the moth and shows her.*

It's dead.
DANIELLA: Yeah.
MARJORIE: So what use is it?
DANIELLA: She keeps me company.
MARJORIE: How can she if she's dead?
DANIELLA: Well at least she was alive once, not like your stupid eyebrows.
> *Pause.*

MARJORIE: You're lucky to have her.
DANIELLA: I know.
MARJORIE: Yeah.
> *Pause.*

DANIELLA: You're not going to pluck them are ya?
MARJORIE: I'm gonna try not to.
DANIELLA: You can't just try, you have to not.
> *Pause.*

MARJORIE: Can I have a loan of Molly?
DANIELLA: What?

MARJORIE: A loan, for overnight. I'd give her back.
DANIELLA: A loan?
MARJORIE: Yeah. To keep me company. So I don't pluck my eyebrows.
DANIELLA: But what will I do?
MARJORIE: It's only for one night.
> *Pause.*

Do you want to see me go to the psych hospital?
DANIELLA: No. Of course not.
MARJORIE: Then lend me Molly.
DANIELLA: I don't know.
MARJORIE: Come on.
DANIELLA: Why should I?
MARJORIE: Please.
> DANIELLA *looks at a the small moth. She strokes it. It is absolutely excruciating for her to give it away.*

DANIELLA: How would you like a little holiday, Molly? You could come straight back. Straight back tomorrow. And it will have been as if you've never even been away. So I'll let you go on this holiday but you must promise to fly straight back.
> MARJORIE *puts her hand out to take the moth.*

> DANIELLA *looks at the moth again and then puts her hand out to transfer it.*

You will give her back?
MARJORIE: Of course I will.
DANIELLA: Promise.
MARJORIE: Swear on the bible.
DANIELLA: Swear on the bible and something else. Something important to you.
> *Pause.*

MARJORIE: Don't have anything else.
DANIELLA: What about your mother's life or something?
> *Pause.*

MARJORIE: Nah.
DANIELLA: Then swear on your own life.
MARJORIE: I swear. Now come on.

DANIELLA *puts out her hand, she puts the moth in* MARJORIE*'s hand. Suddenly* MARJORIE *cries out, jerks her hand up and the moth goes flying across the yard onto the path beyond.*

It fluttered.
DANIELLA: She did not. Now look what you've done.
MARJORIE: I swear to you that it fluttered.
DANIELLA: You did that on purpose.
MARJORIE: I didn't.
DANIELLA: You did. She's right out there. Someone is going to stand on her.
MARJORIE: Keep your voice down, you'll have the guard on top of us.
DANIELLA: You swore. You swore on your own life.
MARJORIE: Yeah. So. So what? It's only a stupid moth.
DANIELLA: You're the stupid one.
MARJORIE: Shut up.
DANIELLA: I hate you. I hate you. I hope you do go to the psych ward.

MRS KAY *walks down the corridor.*

MRS KAY: What do you girls think you're doing?
MARJORIE: Nothing, Mrs Kay.
DANIELLA: Sorry, Mrs Kay.
MRS KAY: Now go back to work.

She turns and stands on the moth. She feels it under her foot and then stamps on it and scrapes it off, kicking it over towards DANIELLA.

DANIELLA *retrieves the little moth and cries over it.*

DANIELLA: I'm sorry. I'm so sorry Molly. I should never have let you go. I'm so sorry.

She continues to cry as MARJORIE *sits down beside her. We see her reach her hand up to her eyebrows and begin to pluck them.*

◆ ◆ ◆ ◆ ◆

SCENE TWENTY-FOUR

GUARD FUREDI *blows a whistle.*

FUREDI: All rise.

The girls who are all on stage together, in the separate cells, rise from their beds. Their clothing is passed to them through a flap which is then relocked. In perfect unison, the girls get out of bed, take off their nightdresses, fold them, tie them with tape and place them with their reading matter on the bed. They get dressed and then stand at the head of the bed. All the cell doors are opened and FUREDI *inspects the beds for tidiness. The* GIRLS, *without exception, have their eyes to the floor.*

Kneel.

The GIRLS, *simultaneously, kneel.*

GIRLS: Our Father,
Who Art in Heaven,
Hallowed be thy name,
Thy kingdom come,
Thy will be done on earth
as it is in heaven.
Give us this day our daily bread
And forgive us our trespasses,
As we forgive those who trespass against us
Lead us not into temptation
But deliver us from evil
For thine is the kingdom, the power and the glory,
For ever and ever,
Amen.

FUREDI: Stand.

The GIRLS, *in unison, stand at attention, facing the bed.*

Gear up.

The GIRLS *pick up their nightwear, night can and reading material.*

Move.

The GIRLS *move to the cabin doorways.*

Daniella Greaves.

DANIELLA: Yes, Mr Furedi.

DANIELLA *goes to her locker, place her night attire on the shelf and picks up her comb and toothbrush. She then moves back to the cell door.*

Reporting back to you Mr Furedi.
FUREDI: Marjorie Linnett.
MARJORIE: Yes, Mr Furedi.

FUREDI checks MARJORIE'S *eyebrows.*

FUREDI: Come with me.
MARJORIE: No. No, please.

FUREDI drags MARJORIE, *kicking and screaming, off. The other* GIRLS *watch.*

MRS KAY, *distressed, takes up the routine.*

MRS KAY: Jane Rogers.
JANE: Yes, Mrs Kay

JANE *goes to her locker, places her night attire on the shelf, picks up her comb and toothbrush. She then moves back to the cell door.*

MRS KAY: Daniella Greaves.
DANIELLA: Yes, Mrs Kay.

DANIELLA *moves to another part of the stage to shower. She empties her night can, uses the toilet, washes and cleans her teeth. When she is finished she returns to* MRS KAY.

Reporting to you, Mrs Kay.
MRS KAY: Carry on.

DANIELLA *collects her cabin cleaning gear, moves to her locker, replaces the comb and toothbrush and then goes back to her cell door.*

As all the GIRLS *go through this routine they will finish one by one and end by standing at their cell doors.* MARJORIE'S *cell door stands ominously ajar.*

The GIRLS *simultaneously take three steps into their cells. The doors are then closed and locked by the officers, but the flap on the cell is left open.*

MRS KAY *comes back and serves breakfast through the flap.*

◆ ◆ ◆ ◆ ◆

SCENE TWENTY-FIVE

The GIRLS *are again in scripture class with* MRS KAY.

MRS KAY: [*reading*] Love is patient, Love is kind,
It does not envy, it does not boast,
It is not proud, It is not rude,
It is not self-seeking,
It is not easily angered,
It keeps no record of wrongs.
Love does not delight in evil,
but rejoices with the truth.
Love always protects, always trusts,
always hopes, always perseveres.
Love bears all things, believes all things,
hopes all things, endures all things.
And now faith hope and love abide, these three; and the greatest of these is love.
  Pause.
JANE: Why does God make people go mad?
MRS KAY: The question of suffering is a complex and difficult area when it comes to God.
JANE: No, straight up. Just why.
MRS KAY: Why is complicated. God doesn't make people go mad.
JANE: I thought God controlled everything.
MRS KAY: God does.
JANE: Then he makes people go mad.
MRS KAY: No.
JANE: Then he doesn't control everything.
MRS KAY: Things happen in the world so that God's love may become apparent. To every bad event there is usually a corollary …
DANIELLA: A what?
MRS KAY: Another thing that is good.
DANIELLA: Where's the good in people going mad?
MRS KAY: Well. I don't know. I don't claim to understand God but perhaps another way to think of it is that it allows other people to show compassion toward the person with the mental illness.
EMMA: Show what?

MRS KAY: Kindness.

JANE: Yeah, right. So God makes people mad so that other people can be nice.

EMMA: Tough luck for the mad person though.

MRS KAY: Girls, I encourage you to question the scriptures. But I counsel you against thinking that just because you can't understand everything it makes it untrue.

DANIELLA: Then how should we know.

MRS KAY: Some things we have to accept on faith.

Pause. The GIRLS *all look at her, unconvinced. Suddenly* JANE *stands up. She overturns her chair.*

JANE: It's not fair.

MRS KAY: Jane. Pick up your chair and sit down.

JANE *looks at her. She goes to the chair and picks it up and hurls it across the space.*

MRS KAY *does not move from where she is sitting. They stare at each other.*

Pick up your chair and sit down.

JANE: Come on. Call the Superintendent on me.

MRS KAY: No.

JANE: Come on. Put me in there too. Put me in there where they're going to put Marjorie. Put me in the mad house as well.

JANE *screams in a rage and then begins to cry.* MRS KAY *goes over to her and gives her a hug.* JANE *quickly composes herself and pushes her away, viciously wiping away her tears.*

Aren't you gonna call the superintendent?

MRS KAY: No. Now pick up your chair and sit down.

JANE *looks at her. Then she retrieves the chair and sits down.*

Marjorie is being sent to the psychiatric home?

DANIELLA: The loony bin.

MRS KAY: Well clearly those who know about these things think she could benefit from the treatment that is offered there.

Pause.

You girls have got to learn to stop being driven by your fears. You know nothing about what happens in the psychiatric home, do you?

EMMA: Only know that we never see those girls ever again.
MRS KAY: Well perhaps that's because they complete their treatment and are released.

Pause.

It is ignorance that feeds your fears.
JANE: No. It's how they took her away.
EMMA: Yeah.
MRS KAY: They had to use force and that scared you?
DANIELLA: They shoved the stuff down her throat.
MRS KAY: What stuff?
EMMA: We dunno. But it made her go all limp.

Pause.

MRS KAY: What did you see?
DANIELLA: Just what I said. They shoved the stuff down her throat.

Pause.

MRS KAY: Show me.
EMMA: Show you what?
MRS KAY: Show me what you saw.

EMMA and DANIELLA go over to JANE. JANE is held down by EMMA and DANIELLA tries to shove the contents of an imaginary bottle down JANE's throat.

JANE struggles but EMMA and DANIELLA use force. After several moments they release JANE. She is woozy and groggy, clearly drugged. JANE staggers around the space disorientated until finally she collapses. Then she gets up and they all return to their seats.

Why would they let you see that?
DANIELLA: Dunno.
EMMA: They just did.

Pause.

MRS KAY: No. Even if they did do that, they wouldn't have let you see it.
JANE: But they did.

Pause.

MRS KAY: Why are you girls making it worse for yourselves?
EMMA: What?
MRS KAY: I'm on your side. I've been on your side from the beginning. Is that why you think you can take advantage of me?
GWEN: She doesn't believe us.
MRS KAY: No. I don't believe you and I'm not going to fall for your tricks.
JANE: But it happened.
DANIELLA: Just like we showed.
EMMA: Marjorie is in the madhouse right now.
FIONA: And you helped put her there.

Pause.

MRS KAY: Eyes to the floor.
JANE: What?
MRS KAY: [*raising her voice*] I said eyes to the floor.

The GIRLS *look down to the floor.*

MRS KAY *sits looking at them. Upset and conflicted by what has transpired but still determined to retain control. She doesn't know what to do next. Then she opens the bible and finds a passage to read.*

[*Reading*] Resist the devil and he will flee from you. Draw near to God, and he will draw near to you. Cleanse your hands you sinners, and purify your hearts, you double-minded. Humble yourselves before God who will exalt you.

♦ ♦ ♦ ♦ ♦

SCENE TWENTY-SIX

JANE *is in the centre of the room while the other* GIRLS *are in a bunch at the side. As* JANE *walks the others move but when she turns around they are still. Essentially she is playing a game of shadows with them. She looks at them.*

JANE: When you are in your cell at night. All by yourself. Sometimes your mind plays tricks. [*She turns around and continues to walk, not looking at the 'days'.*] Who's there?

DAY 1: You know.
JANE: Who's there? Hello?
DAY 2: You know who brays.
DAY 3: We're your wasted days.
DAY 4: You know who fights.
DAY 5: We're your wasted nights.

She turns and looks but again they are frozen. She looks at them.

JANE: When you are in your cell at night. All by yourself. Sometimes your mind plays games.

She turns and walks again, not looking at the 'days'.

What do you want?
DAY 1: You know.
JANE: What do you want? Hello?
DAY 2: You keep getting put away.
DAY 3: We're the ones who pay.
DAY 4: You keep getting shut in.
DAY 5: We're the ones who don't win.
JANE: What do you want me to do?
DAY 1: Learn to sneak.
DAY 2: Learn to hide.
DAY 3: Be nice to their face.
DAY 4: But keep your feelings inside.
DAY 5: Fly under the radar.
DAY 1: And don't get sprung.
DAY 2: Pretend to be good.
DAY 3: So that we can have fun.

She turns and looks at the frozen 'days'.

JANE: When you are in your cell at night. All by yourself. Sometimes your figure out how the world works.

She turns and walks around her cell.

DAY 1: You're a rebel.
DAY 2: You're in trouble.
DAY 3: No-one tells you what to do.
DAY 4: But the more you buck the system.
DAY 5: The more they punish you.
DAY 1: We want you to stay a rebel.

DAY 2: We want you to keep your guts.
DAY 3: But you have to pull your punches.
DAY 4: And you have to choose your puts.

She turns and looks at them.

JANE: When you are in your cell at night. All by yourself. Sometimes you learn how to fake it. How to fake being nice. How to fake being sweet. How to fake being obedient. So that you can get out of here, and out of their clutches and away from the people who want to tell you what to do and how to do it. And you learn, and you learn the hard way, that a girl has to appear to be one thing and hide deep down inside what she really is and what she can let herself become once she gets out of here.

The days all hug around her. JANE *hugs her arms around herself and paces her cell.*

♦ ♦ ♦ ♦ ♦

SCENE TWENTY-SEVEN

EMMA *is carrying a tray to* GWEN, *who is in solitary confinement. She puts it down and stares at her.*

GWEN: What do you call this?

EMMA *looks at her.* GWEN *takes something out of her hair.*

EMMA: A nit.
GWEN: Yeah. But what do you call it?
EMMA: Thinil.
GWEN: And a louse?
EMMA: Kapul.
GWEN: And a maggot?
EMMA: Nhukuy.

GWEN *nods.* EMMA *sits down.*

GWEN: What's the word for sister?

EMMA *shakes her head.*

Don't you know it?
EMMA: Kapu.
GWEN: What's that?

EMMA: That's the word for any small creature you haven't got a name for.

   Pause.

GWEN: Like an insect.

EMMA: Yeah, like anything that gives you the creeps.

   Pause. They laugh.

  Kaathii.

GWEN: Is that how you say us?

EMMA: Kaathii. That's how you say sister.

   EMMA *exits.*

GWEN: Kaathii.

◆ ◆ ◆ ◆ ◆

SCENE TWENTY-EIGHT

NAYLOR *enters,* GWEN *looks to the floor.*

NAYLOR: You're being transferred, Gill, back to Parramatta. We're done with you here. You will be given time to pack up your things and then you will be transported back to Sydney.

   There is silence. GWEN *gradually raises her eyes to* NAYLOR.

GWEN: I don't want to go back to Sydney.

NAYLOR: Eyes to the floor.

   But GWEN *does not put her eyes to the floor.*

NAYLOR: I said, eyes to the floor.

   Still, GWEN *looks at him.*

   NAYLOR *comes close to her, threateningly close. She meets his eye.*

GWEN: [*a small voice*] You don't own me.

   NAYLOR *raises his hand to strike her, but hesitates.*

   [*Hesitantly but with increasing confidence*] 'Cause how would you explain the bruises? 'Cause there's a medical check when you enter Parramatta and the doctor would have to note them down wouldn't he? Then they'd be on the record wouldn't they?

   NAYLOR *stares at her. He folds his arms.*

NAYLOR: So, you've got something left, have you Gill?
GWEN: Have I?
> *He walks around her.*

NAYLOR: There's a way that the world works. Everywhere you go. There's a way that the world works. And those who agree to its conditions, those who subscribe to its rules, they succeed. They can even rail against it or poke fun at it or seem to be rebelling, but they only go far enough not to get into real trouble. And we tolerate them, because they know the limits. Then there are people like you Gill, who see the way that the world works and say, 'I'm not gonna do that, I'm smarter than that, I'm better than that, I'm going to do whatever I want.' And you're the ones who end up in here. And you suffer and you hurt and you're more and more controlled but for some reason, for some reason, you continue to rebel.
GWEN: For some reason?
NAYLOR: Yes, for some reason that is beyond our comprehension. For some reason you can't just see the way the world works and behave.
> *Pause.*

GWEN: Because I'm bad?
NAYLOR: I'm afraid so.
GWEN: I can't see how the world works and so I rebel?
NAYLOR: That's what I believe.
GWEN: And what else have you left me?
NAYLOR: I'm sorry?
GWEN: I said, what else have you left for me except that?
NAYLOR: [*amused*] What have I left you? Because it's always about me, isn't it, Gill? The problem is always with me, isn't it?
GWEN: Yeah.
NAYLOR: You could have your freedom, you could have your own life back.
GWEN: If I do as I'm told?
NAYLOR: Yes.
GWEN: Really?
NAYLOR: Really.
> *Pause.*

GWEN: Could I go back to Carowa?

NAYLOR: Possibly.
GWEN: That's where I was born.
NAYLOR: If you learn to do as you're told.
> GWEN *stares at him for a long moment.*

Eyes to the floor.
> GWEN *looks at him, silently. Her eyes begin to fill with tears.*

Eyes to the floor.
> GWEN *very slowly, with great difficulty, lowers her eyes to the floor.*

Thank you, Gill. Keep that up and you're be back to Cowra in no time.
GWEN: Carowa.
NAYLOR: Carowa, sir.
GWEN: Carowa, sir.
> GWEN *is crying, sobbing almost uncontrollably.*

NAYLOR: It will be hard at first Gwen, it will be very hard. But you've taken the first step to being part of something much bigger than you. To being part of your society. And you'll find, if you persist, that society will accept you if you accept it. We are not hard on everyone, only the one's who won't fit. Only the ones who won't fit. [*Beat.*] Now stop that blubbering and run along.
> GWEN *exits, still crying, past the other* GIRLS.

SCENE TWENTY-NINE

The GIRLS *all line up on stage, in formation for muster. They directly address the audience.*

NAYLOR: When you leave here, girls, you will be charged with becoming good citizens of this great nation. You will be given a small stipend and you will be encouraged to take your place as the mothers and wives of Australia. I encourage you to do so. You will be interested to know that your transformation here has been a matter for the State Parliament of NSW and I quote. The girls who have been transferred to Hay have all benefited quite markedly from the experience and upon their return to Parramatta have displayed attitudes and a general demeanour of a satisfactory standard.

HAWKINS: My under-secretary and the officer in charge of the establishment division recently visited Hay and spoke with those difficult girls who hitherto would have been sent to Long Bay.

FIONA: They sent me to Long Bay. And all I can tell you is that it was a lot nicer than Hay. This place. This place was ... [*She breaks down crying.*] I can't tell you how bad it was. But it was brutal. And I carried it with me ... all my life. All through my life I carried it. I'm still carrying it.

HAWKINS: Following their most recent visit I received an excellent report from these officers. They asked the girls whether they had any message for their mates at Parramatta.

MARJORIE: I was returned to Parramatta and committed to the psychiatric wing of the Parramatta psych home. They didn't hold me there for long. When I got out I went up the Cross and lived on the streets for a while. Worked for a while. Had a couple of kids. But they're with their father now. I've seen them a bit since they got older. Been in and out of psychiatric care most of my life. Don't know what else to say. I'm nothing special. Turns out, I'm just a silly old bugger. But I still don't think I deserved none of this.

HAWKINS: Many of the girls had nothing to say, but one of them said, 'Yes, tell them that this place stinks and whatever they do, don't come down here'. Hay was established to create just that sort of feeling.

JANE: Institutionalisation has a multigenerational effect. My mother was institutionalised with the Sisters of Mercy. My father was in one of them institutions where they worked on a farm, and he was horrendously abused. My daughter is the first in three generations to stay with her mum. It has been a constant struggle for me and she will have effects and she does have effects. My children all have drug problems from time to time with one son being in constant incarceration.

MRS KAY: The staff were just people like me. We had no special training. Though I was a trained nurse so I supposed I was one up. The men who worked there were just ordinary fellows from around Hay. The women were the same, they were just housewives, who could spare the time from their commitments so they could take the job. We were not given any real instructions, except, 'Make them behave, don't let them talk.'

DANIELLA: The health care needs of those of us who remain as survivors of this infamous institution are overwhelming. The majority of our people suffer from varying degrees of mental illness. Post traumatic stress disorder is one thing we all seem to have in common. Depression and anxiety related illnesses such as panic attacks and sleep disorders are common, as are some phobic disorders.

MRS KAY: I was transferred to Condoblin and never went back to Hay. It was really just an accident of geography that I was ever in Hay at all. I guess that's a bit the same for the people who lived in Hay when I did. It wasn't up to them that these girls were here. This place, it was something that was done to Hay, and to me as well. That's what I want to be able to admit to myself. So I can look into the face of the horror and say, this was something that was done to me as well.

NAYLOR: I just want to say that hindsight is always 20/20 vision. At the time we did what we could to discipline them. We thought discipline was the only thing we could give them.

GWEN: You stole our childhood, you stole our lives.

NAYLOR: Emma Abbot, step out.

> EMMA *steps out.*

The rest of you. Shoulders back. Eyes to the Floor. And quick march.

> *The* GIRLS *process off.* NAYLOR *follows them.* EMMA *walks forward, addressing the audience.*

EMMA: I never saw my sister again. By the time I got out she'd just disappeared. I went looking in all the correctional facilities because one out of six of us are likely to end up in those places. I went looking at the mental hospitals because you know one in three of us are likely to attempt suicide. I don't know if that's why I couldn't find her. I still hope that one day I might know. But right now, today, she is still missing. People think that what happened here, it's in the past. Um. I just want to say, it's just not.

> EMMA *exits the stage.*
>
> *Lights fade.*

ALSO BY ALANA VALENTINE

The Conjurers
ISBN 978-0-86819-510-0

Cyberbile & Grounded
ISBN 978-0-86819-984-9

Run Rabbit Run
ISBN 978-0-86819-747-0

Savage Grace and Love Potions
ISBN 978-0-97755-020-3

Shafana and Aunt Sarrinah
ISBN 978-0-86819-882-8

Singing the Lonely Heart and Ozone
978-0-97755-021-0

Swimming the Globe
ISBN 978-0-86819-595-7

For these and other Australian plays,
visit our website:
www.currency.com.au

www.ingramcontent.com/pod-product-compliance
Lightning Source LLC
Chambersburg PA
CBHW060929180426
43192CB00044B/2836